Birman Cats

A Birman Cat Pet Owner's Guide

Birman Cat Basics, Choosing and Owning, Breeding, Care, Nutrition, Grooming, Showing and Training All Included!

By: Lolly Brown

Copyrights and Trademarks

Disclaimer and Legal Notice

Foreword

This instructional guide will discuss all of the things that you need to know in order to get started with raising training your new Birman cat. Bringing home a new addition for the first time can be a really exciting endeavor. The whole family may have spent time picking out the kitten that they wanted to bring home, and now they are excited to bond with him and to make some lasting memories.

This guidebook is going to walk you through the steps that you need to follow in order to raise your Birman cat well, get your cat trained and ready to behave.

Included inside this book's first section is about the origin and bio of a Birman cat. It also contains information about its appearance, personality, behavior and lifespan.

The Second section is about choosing a Birman cat. It tackles about where and how to acquire a Birman cat and how to select a healthy Birman kitten.

The next section will talk about the things that you need and have to do as a Birman cat owner.

The fourth section focuses on how you can cater your cat's nutritional needs.

The next section delves into basic care and regular grooming needs for your Birman cat.

The sixth section is about raising and training your Birman cat. It educates cat owners about the importance of training and activities for your Birman cat. It additionally contains a cat's training outline and guidance in shaping behaviors, training, and problem solving.

Th seventh section focuses on the common health issues and how to deal with them.

Chapter eight is about preparing your Birman cat for a show and things to consider if you have to travel your cat.

For the last section, it will talk about the breeding process for your Birman cat.

By obtaining this training guide, you will be on your way to securing the necessary tools and knowledge to assure your success as a cat owner and trainer.

Table of Contents

Introduction

Having a pet is among the most fulfilling and occasionally among the most difficult undertakings that any individual can get involved in. Research studies demonstrate that having a pet can dramatically decrease stress levels and can play a dynamic part in psychosocial growth for kids and grownups. Many individuals have even had their lives saved by the pets they look after, which goes for practically any kind of pet.

In this book, we're going to be talking all about Birman cats to assist you to pick a brand-new feline buddy and care for him/her!

Initially, we'll go over the general information about Birman cats and some credible locations where you can obtain a brand-new Birman cat and exactly how to set about choosing the cat that ideally suits your character. After that, we'll look at the standard vet needs that all brand-new Birman cats should have. Afterward, we'll go over behavioral and social training for your Birman cat, taking care of your cat when it ends up being sick or hurt, and exactly how to expand the life of your pet with a healthy diet plan and activities.

Let's get started.

Chapter One: Birman Cat Origin and Characteristics

History

A Birman cat has a lovely legend of origin. The Sacred Cat of Burma, as the Birman is every now and then called, is stated to have obtained his putting look via the intervention of a blue-eyed goddess, who rewarded a temple cat's love for and devotion to his priest via turning his white coat golden and altering his yellow eyes to blue. As an image of his purity, his paws remained white. Ever since, the temple cats have borne the goddess's marks of favor, and it was once stated that monks who died have been reborn into the cats' bodies.

How the cats certainly got here to be is unknown. Theories encompass crosses of Siamese with Angoras or Persians, however when or the place these unique meetups took place is unknown. They may additionally have taken region in southeast Asia, between a variety of cats who carried the genes for a pointed pattern, lengthy hair and blue eyes, or the breed might also have been created in France from cats imported by way of two Europeans, a Frenchman named Auguste Pavie, and a Major Gordon Russell, who had been given a pair of temple cats in 1919 as a reward for assisting the priests. The cats had been shipped to France, however the male did no longer make it there alive. Before he died, however, he had impregnated the female, and her kittens helped to set up the breed in Europe. It used to be diagnosed in France in 1925 as the Sacre de Birmanie, from which comes the contemporary breed name, Birman.

The cats have been first imported to the United States in 1959 and had been identified by using the Cat Fanciers Association in 1967. They are additionally diagnosed through the American Cat Fanciers Association, the Canadian Cat Association, the Cat Fanciers Federation and The International Cat Association.

Appearance

Birmans are medium-sized cats with a wide, round face and a Roman nose. Their eyes are definitely spherical in structure and are deep blue or sapphire blue in color. Their breed is now not definitely black in color or coat however the most frequent cats in this breed do have black markings on their faces. Their fur is fairly lengthy and is pretty silky. Their ears are symmetrical to the relaxation of their face and their ears are located between the pinnacle and facet of their heads.

The most fascinating function of this cat breed is the 'gloves' on their feet. They have a unique coloration marking on their ft which makes it appear like the cats are carrying white gloves on their body. While their physique coat and face would possibly be of a single color, in the main white, their paws are every now and then extraordinary colorations such as black, brown, or blue. These contrasting 'gloves' are a special characteristic alongside with their blue eyes.

Birmans additionally come in one-of-a-kind point hues like chocolate, red, cream, or even lilac. Tabby and Tortie coat sorts of Birman cats can additionally be found. Birman kittens are born with a pure white coat on their physique which includes on their paws, ears, and ft and they have blue eyes as well.

Size

Birmans normally weigh 6 to 12 pounds.

Personality

If you like the pointed sample of the Siamese but no longer the yowly voice, a Birman may be the cat for you. He is a submissive, quiet cat who loves human beings and will observe them from room to room. Expect the Birman cat to prefer to be concerned in what you're doing, and be appreciative that he's now not as bossy as the Siamese.

Docile doesn't imply dumb. The Birman is a clever cat and, certainly, curious. He likes to discover his surroundings and has been observed to get trapped under flooring that are being altered or to by accident (maybe on purpose) go for a ride on pinnacle of a car. It's a top thought to continuously preserve tabs on the place he is.

He communicates in a tender voice, mostly to remind you that possibly it's time for dinner or perhaps for a first-rate cuddle on the sofa. He loves being held and will loosen up in your palms like a furry baby.

Lifespan

The common lifespan of a Birman cat is thirteen to 15 years.

Chapter Two: Choosing a Birman Cat

When you buy a cat, it usually happens one of two ways: either (a) it is carefully planned, or (b) it is totally spontaneous.

One of those ways happens when you research breeds and look into what type of cat you want, start talking to breeders or shops in your local area and wait for a litter to be born and weaned.

The other way, which, let's face it, is more likely, happens when you walk past a pet shop and see a cute face staring at you in the window. Before you know what has happened, you find yourself sitting at home on the kitchen floor with a new kitten on a blanket, wondering what to feed her and where she is going to sleep!

Don't worry; we have all been there and done that, captured by the forlorn gaze of a lonely animal in a pet-store window. But if you can manage it, the best way to expand your family into pet ownership is to plan for it properly.

However, even when you do plan for it, there is still a right way and a wrong way to go about buying a cat

The Wrong Way

The "wrong way" includes: answering a classified ad in the local paper, buying a cat out of the back of a truck at the market, and even taking a free kitten off somebody-who-knows-somebody at work.

You can tell I am not a fan of these cat buying methods. Why? Well, because you just don't know what you are getting and putting it bluntly, you are often being duped. It is highly likely that someone is taking money off you to offload a cat that they have been unable to sell via a legitimate channel for some reason.

A cat that is acquired in any of these ways is, more than likely, going to have some kind of problem. You just don't know what it is yet, so you don't know what hassle you are getting yourself into.

Diseases are common, but of more concern are poor quality cross-bred animals that have some kind of genetic abnormality that causes health problems later on.

What you need to consider is that when you purchase a cat, you are investing two things: you are not just investing money; you are also investing your heart. So, you need to ask yourself, "Do I really want to get myself emotionally attached to an unhealthy animal that I am going to have to watch suffer later on?"

And it will cost you financially too. If you think you are saving money by buying a cat cheaply, you are not. It is a false economy. Once your heart is invested, and you have formed a loving bond with your new best friend, you are going to want to do whatever you can to help them if and when they get sick. And expensive vet bills are the price you will have to pay for skimping on the initial cost of a good quality animal.

A final point to consider here is the effect it can have on your children. When you bring a pet home, it becomes a member of your family. Your children bond with it, and it becomes their best friend. But if that beloved family pet was never healthy in the first place and gets sick or dies after just a few months or even a couple of years, it can be very traumatizing. You can avoid all that heartache by doing the right thing in the first place.

In my opinion, even picking up a cat from the local Pound is preferable to the options above. Although once again, you do not know what you are getting, and with a "Pound cat," you could be bringing home an animal with behavioral issues.

The Right Way

The "proper way," or at least a better way, to buy a cat, is to buy from a breeder, or a reputable pet shop, or even from your local vet.

Breeder

Cats from breeders will come from healthy stock. They will be genetically sound and have no abnormalities that can cause problems as the cat grows. Most States or jurisdictions have certification processes for Breeders, with specific standards and requirements that the Breeder needs to meet. This guarantees that you get a healthy kitten that has the best chance of growing up strong and won't develop issues once it is an adult. Buying a cat from a breeder is more expensive initially but is worth it in the long run. You ensure for yourself that you are getting a healthy animal that has the best chance of a long, happy life. Your family deserves that.

Pet Shop

Cats from Pet Shops should be the same, as long as you go to a well-established decent-sized store. Larger shops usually get their stock directly from breeders. They will establish good relationships with many reputable local breeders to ensure that they always have a constant supply of healthy stock for their store.

You should be able to tell where the stock is coming from just by talking with the staff in the store. Just ask how many weeks old the cat is and how long the cat has been in the store, and you will start to get an understanding of where it has come from. You will often see a whole litter of the same animal in the store when the stock has come from a breeder.

Beware, though; not all pet stores are the same. Small, independent stores should be okay in general, but beware if a store seems to be showing signs that it is struggling. In such cases, they might not be buying quality stock from breeders and be getting any animals they can from less reliable sources. When this is the case, you usually find that they might only have single animals rather than a litter, and generally only a few animals in the whole store.

Vet

It is not always the first thought that comes to mind for most people, as we tend to think of vets as places to "fix" pets rather than acquire them, but your local vet may often have animals for sale. And if not, they will at least be able to point you in the right direction. Talking to your local vet is undoubtedly the easiest and quickest way to get useful information about the supply of pets in your local area. They will know who the good breeders are and which pet shops are the best for getting quality animals. Chatting with a vet is definitely a good information gathering exercise to do before you decide where to buy.

The Pound or Pet Shelter

As mentioned earlier, I am in two minds about buying a cat from a Pound or Pet Shelter. On the one hand, you show yourself to be a good citizen by adopting an unwanted animal with no home. It is all very altruistic and certainly helps society, and I understand that is a good thing.

But on the other hand, you don't know why they have ended up in the shelter, and often they may have behavioral issues. Adopting a mature cat is a very different experience than adopting a kitten, and you need to be prepared to "take what you get," just as you would when adopting a teenage child. So, if you get a mature cat from a Shelter, you need to be ready for what may be a wild ride as they adapt to a situation that may be very different from what they are used to. It may be a while before they fully settle into their new home environment.

I also understand that for many people, when funds are short, getting a cat from a Shelter may be the only economically viable option. So, if you do buy from a shelter, just ask as many questions as possible and try to find out as much as you can about that particular pet and their background. That will hopefully help you avoid bringing home a cat with issues.

How Old?

Once a litter of cats is born, the kittens stay close to their mother, being dependent on her for milk, warmth, and comfort. But by about eight weeks, the kittens will have been weaned and be eating solid food.

Ideally, they should then stay with the mother for a few more weeks to keep growing and become more confident. Kittens are growing very rapidly at this stage, and every few days that pass are equivalent to a few months of human growth.

This eight-to-twelve-week period is like the toddler stage for humans; and although we might put our toddlers in nursery or childcare for a few hours whilst we work, we don't usually start sending our kids off to spend a full day at primary school until they are past that toddler stage. The same with kittens, it's good for them to start playing and exploring away from their mother at this age, but they are a bit young to leave her and be adopted by a human family, just yet.

So, if you are buying from a breeder, try and arrange to leave them with the breeder until twelve weeks, even if you already have arranged the purchase. However, you can't do that with a pet shop kitten as the kittens will have already left their mother. It is quite common for kittens to arrive in pet shops at around nine or ten weeks. And I think that is okay; after all, pet shops need to make money, and it's easier to sell kittens the smaller and cuter they are. But I just think that overall, it is better for their all-round social development if they don't leave their mother and go off alone to start their new independent lives until they reach twelve weeks.

How To Select A Cat

"Which one do I choose?"

That is a big question.

- What should you look for when selecting a cat?
- How do you know which one is going to be the best?

The main thing you want to look for when choosing a kitten is Personality. Cute looks are fine, but at the end of the day, you need a cat that you feel a connection to and want to spend time with.

Whatever the situation, either at the breeder's home or the pet shop, you should have a chance to look at the litter and interact with them when trying to choose one. Look for one with an open personality: one that is playful and inquisitive, but not too rambunctious. You want to find the middle ground between not too aggressive and not too shy or timid.

If you can, get down on the floor to be at the same level as them. See whether one naturally comes to you. Try and offer them a toy to see if they are not too shy to reach out and take it, and play with them a little. Try caressing them on the top of their head with the back of your hand.

After a few minutes, pick them up. See if they are happy to let you hold them without struggling to get away or bite you.

While you are doing this, be asking questions of the breeder or shop assistant. Try and find out as much as you can about the kittens' history and find out what the seller has already noticed about each kitten's particular personality.

Once you find a kitten that you seem to connect with, check it over to make sure it looks healthy. You obviously won't know too much about cat health yet, but just be aware of any obvious signs of anything, like patches of fur missing or any rashes or scars. Note whether they look too fat or too skinny compared to others in the litter; a healthy kitten should be neither. Feel their tummy and make sure that it doesn't feel hard or swollen, which could indicate worms. Run your finger through their fur and check for fleas etc. Take your time; don't rush the process. Remember, you are going to have this pet in your family for many years to come.

When you find the right one, though, you will just "know" it. They say it is as much about the cat choosing you as it is about you choosing them, and once they have chosen you, your heart is going to feel it.

Chapter Three: Owning a Birman Cat

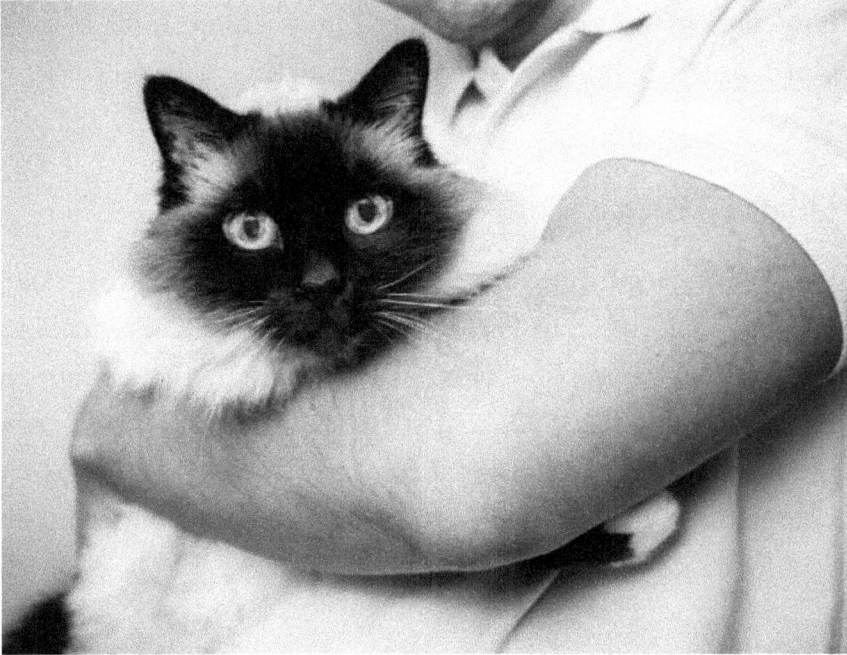

Get Yourself Ready for Pet Ownership

Prior to you even picking a cat, you have to think about whether you're truly prepared to be a cat owner. Generally, cats are relatively low-maintenance compared to some more spectacular pets. For one, there are monetary factors to consider: cats' cost, they have medical expenditures, they consume food, and depending upon where you live, they utilize litter regularly. After the financial resources, you need to consider your allergic reactions and make certain you're either not allergic or choose a cat that does not set off your allergic reactions. You additionally have to have the correct quantity of time to purchase your brand-new feline buddy or buddies. It appears like a great deal of work on paper; however, many people discover that owning a cat is well worth any expenditures that are included.

Financial Preparation

Cats need things, and much of those things cost cash. For one, cats have to eat. We'll go over particular feeding techniques later on; however, let's simply state that usually, it is going to cost about $25 a month to feed your cat (a little can of food a day plus additional dry food). For every single cat you include, you can add $15-$20 monthly. Cats additionally require standard vet attention, such as shots.

The expense of these depends upon your neighborhood veterinarian; however, you can most likely anticipate to pay between $20 and $50 for shots and upwards of $50 for spaying and neutering. Fortunately, if you choose to get your cat from a shelter, they are going to typically make certain the cat is spayed or sterilized for you. You then need to think about things like cat toys, tick and flea control, preventative worm medication, training aids, litter, and so on. All and all, a great price quote is between $300 and $700 a year.

Cats are infamously independent, and many individuals have actually owned cats gladly without numerous expensive things. Just the same, you're facing a minimum of $300 a year simply for the standard requirements and $500-$ 800 in overall expenses for the initial year of owning a cat. The initial year costs more since there are more medical costs, and you might need to spend for spaying or neutering.

So, as you can see, it's not exceptionally economically taxing, however, if it may be too much for your budget, then you ought to seriously think about getting a cat. Veterinarian care and vaccines are where the majority of people attempt to spare cash when owning a cat (or any animal). The unfortunate reality is that the absence of veterinary care considerably lowers the life span of cats. With appropriate care, a lot of mixed-breed cats can live upwards of 18 years! Without appropriate care, the life span diminishes to 11-12 years, and "feral" or "wild" cats that live outdoors and have a very little owner or veterinary care have a frighteningly brief life span of just a couple of years.

Pedigree additionally enters into play here. Purebred cats have a tendency to have more congenital defects and problems. They additionally come along with considerably greater expenses! Your veterinarian expenses for a purebred cat might be triple or quadruple of your expenses for a mixed breed! Take this into consideration prior to adopting a brand-new animal.

Time Management

Statistically, cats are the leading choice for individuals who have degrees and professional jobs. Is that due to the fact that cats are naturally wise or that classy individuals are drawn to them? Perhaps, however, the most likely explanation is that cats are exceptionally independent. Individuals with those sorts of dedications most likely do not have the energy or time to own a high-maintenance animal like a dog. That being stated, you can't simply purchase a cat, and after that, leave it in your home all the time and rarely have contact with it.

Cats require human contact to keep healthy habits and mindsets towards people and other animals. Your future cat is going to more than happy simply walking around your home, doing as she or he pleases. However, like any living thing, cats require company. If you work a full-time job and do not have a great deal of time to focus on your animal when you get home, then you might wish to reassess owning one, specifically if there's nobody at home when you're gone.

In some cases, we can't truly manage where we work, however, the desire for a furry buddy is still there; you can make it work. This is why I typically suggest getting at least 2 cats. A single-cat home can work out; however, having sister or brother cats or cats that have actually matured together is the ideal setting. The cats are going to have contact with one another and with people; the included advantage is that they get to have fun with one another when you do not have time to play.

This is going to keep your cats from going stir-crazy when you need to go to work daily and can't be with them. A two-cat home is more costly and needs more work to preserve, however, cats are social animals and are going to have a far better lifestyle if they have their own feline buddies to socialize with.

Supplies to Prepare

In taking care of a Birman cat, you have to keep in mind that there are certain supplies you need to have with you—to make sure that his stay in your house would be easy and smooth-sailing. This means that you have to have the following:

Food

You have to make sure that the Birman cat has been weaned before taking him home. You have to make sure that both wet and dry food are at home, and that there also should be plenty of fresh water. It would be good to feed at scheduled times. Free-feeding is not encouraged because it lessens your hold on the cat—and makes him somehow stubborn.

Be mindful about mixing what you want the kitten to eat with what he's already used to eating. This way, you won't have a hard time introducing new food to him, and you can avoid him from suffering from stomach upset.

One thing to keep in mind is that you should avoid foods that contain tuna, corn, or other grains. Tuna has high mercury content, while corn and grains would do nothing good for your cat. Forego the food if you see that tuna, soy, grains, or corn are part of the ingredients—in short, you do have to read food labels.

Cow's milk should also be avoided. This isn't good for cats—no matter what the breed. This is because cow's milk cannot be easily digested and may even cause diarrhea, so if you want to feed the cat with milk, choose lactose-free ones that you can get from your local pet stores.

Meanwhile, if you're going to feed the cat with refrigerated food, make sure that you heat it first, and stir it thoroughly before letting the cat eat it so that the food would not burn their mouths.

Treats are also good—as long as you make sure that they make up only 10% of your cat's diet. If you give the Birman cat treats after they eat each time, he would look forward to this—and won't try to ask more food from you.

Leashes and Collars

If you're going to use a collar, always check if it still fits your cat right—or if it's becoming too tight.

If you're going to walk the cat, always make sure to use a leash and a harness. Collars might suffocate them—and that's not what you'd want to happen. Never walk your Birman cat on crowded places or busy highways to avoid agitating him.

Litterbox

If you don't want to do the scooping yourself, you can choose a litterbox that has automatic cleaning mechanisms. You can choose ones that have the following features:

- Plastic privacy tents to contain the litter;
- Odorless/Scented ones;
- Lightweight litterboxes;
- Carbon filters—so bad odors could be reduced, especially those that could work even for months;
- Quiet—or does not make any unnecessary sounds;
- Clumping litter use;
- Removable parts—so it would be easy to arrange again;
- Time-saving mechanisms;
- Metal designs, and;
- Those that work on AC Adaptors.

Of course, it would also be important to choose the most affordable ones—so that you'd also get to save some money!

Metal or China Dishes

Metal or China bowls or dishes are recommended because plastic bowls could be quite toxic for cats—and don't have positive effects, even over time.

Flea Combs

Flea Combs are fine toothed combs that prevent fleas from invading your cat's coat. Don't be scared of combing your Birman cat because more often than not, they actually like the feeling of being combed because it's soothing to them—and it's reminiscent of how their mothers used to lick them when they were still part of their litter.

Metal Combs

Meanwhile, metal combs are perfect for making sure that your Birman cat's hair stays healthy and shiny at all times. Choose those that are at least 9 to 12 teeth per inch so you could easily take care of your cat's coat.

Flea Shampoo, Powder, and Spray

Of course, as Birman cats are hairy, furry cats, it's best to make sure that you have flea shampoos, powders, and sprays to make sure they would not get infested with fleas and other coat problems that could make them itch like crazy.

If these are not readily available, you can try squeezing some fresh lemon juice on the flea comb, and use it to comb the cat with. The reason for this is that fleas hate the smell of lemon—which means that they could easily be repelled with this. You can also try giving the cat an apple cider vinegar bath, or simply wipe his coat with the ACV mixed with water. This is especially effective for kittens.

You can also try using hard-shelled algae shampoo, and use a soap with water trap to scrub the cat's room with so fleas could go away.

Scratching Post

A scratching post is essential for your Birman cat—so that he could release his boredom, and the post could also help him declaw—so you'd have less to worry about. Look for ones that have the following features:

- Neutrally toned—so it would look natural;
- Can withstand carpeted floors—or even posts;
- Those with 16" x 16" bases;
- Those that are at least 32" in height;
- Woven and durable sisals;
- Those that are constructed with heavy wood;
- Those with replaceable toys—for extra entertainment;
- Easy set-up mounting systems, or;
- Those with dangling plush toys.

Cat Trees

Cat trees are also great because not only do they give the cat a chance to scratch, cat trees also allow them to have someplace to sit and observe their surroundings—because it is a cat's natural instinct to do so.

Place it near the window, or somewhere they could watch over a room—so they'd feel confident and would really want to stay with you!

Toys

Of course, it is important to keep your Birman cat preoccupied—especially when you are not at home. The best toys for Birman cats these days include:

- Bergan Turbo Scratcher Cat Toy;
- Da Bird Super Pack—including single pole cat toy, sparkly attachment, feather refill, and peacock feather;
- Cat Charmers;
- Hypno Mice Cat Toys;
- Kitty Play Tunnels;
- Interactive Laser Pet Toys;
- Peek-a-Prize Cats;
- Colorful Cat Springs;
- Kong Squirrels, and;
- Cat Nip Toys

Having great toys around would keep your furry feline entertained—and happy, at all times!

Nail Clippers

Nail Clippers also help in grooming the cat—and making sure he doesn't hurt anyone with his claws!

Cat Carrier

And of course, you need to have a good and sturdy cat carrier with you. This is for times when you have to take the cat to the vet, or when you want to take him out with you and he's not trained to walk on a leash yet.

Choose ones that are:

- Stylish but sturdy;
- Come with fleece travel beds or blankets;
- Come with storage pockets;
- Those that come with wired windows;
- Those that are molded, and;
- Those with plenty of ventilation, of course.

Keep these supplies in handy and it would be easy for you to take care of your Birman cat!

Chapter Four: Feeding Your Birman Cat

Your Birman cat requires appropriate nutrients necessary for body development, growth and general function of the body. These nutrients reside in the food that you feed your cat on. Failure to feed your Birman cat on nutritious food stuffs definitely leads to specific nutrient-deficiency illnesses/diseases, some that are obviously life-threatening.

Just in the same way that you pay close attention to what you eat, you also need to pay close attention to what you feed your Birman cat on and in particular when it comes to food composition, which informs nutritional value of the food.

Of all nutrients, water is probably the most important nutrient that your cat needs, although it cannot survive on water alone. The fact that a big percentage of your cat's body weight is literally made up of water makes it very necessary that you supply your cat with fresh drinking water on a daily basis. Lack of water in the body does not only interfere with smooth metabolism; it can also be a cause of serious illnesses.

Your Birman cat also needs a sufficient amount of protein. Protein plays a very important role in the body and in particular in the formation of body cells, tissues, enzymes, organs, antibodies, enzymes and hormones. Your cat's body also requires protein for repair of body tissues and proper maintenance of the body.

Closely related to protein are amino acids that your cat also requires. Amino acids are literally the building blocks of proteins and while your cat's body can easily synthesize non-essential amino acids from its diet, its body cannot naturally synthesize such essential amino acid as taurine, which makes it necessary for your cat's food to contain the same.

Your Birman cat does not only require water and protein. It also requires fats. Fats are very important when it comes to production of specific hormones and in cell structure. Fats are also required by the body for proper utilization of certain vitamins. The food you feed your cat on must contain such essential fats as linoleic and arachidonic acids. Lack of these fats can easily lead to your cat suffering from reduced growth and skin problems.

As has already been indicated elsewhere, Birman cats are very playful and therefore require a lot of energy to remain active. This is why you need to feed your Birman cat on carbohydrates. Carbohydrates do not only provide your cat's body with the energy it requires; carbohydrates play a critical role in maintaining good health of the intestine. You do, however, need to note that cats are generally carnivorous animals and therefore need very little amount of carbohydrates.

Vitamins are the other very important nutrients that your cat needs. Different vitamins play different roles in the body with some vitamins required for enzyme reaction. Since your cat's body cannot synthesize most vitamins, it is very necessary that the food you feed your cat on contains all the required vitamins. Like with the other nutrients, lack of vitamins leads to occurrence of various vitamin-deficiency illnesses.

Lastly, your cat requires sufficient supply of minerals for proper bone and teeth development, for metabolic processes and for maintenance of appropriate fluid balance within the body. Because your cat's body cannot synthesize minerals, you must ensure that your cat food contains these vital inorganic compounds. Although your cat definitely needs different nutrients to grow and remain healthy, the amount of nutrients you feed your cat is very critical. This is so because cats require different amounts of nutrients depending on their age. Birman cats in particular require to be fed on premium food stuffs.

Kitten Nutrition

You definitely have no role to play when it comes to feeding kittens with nutrients. Kittens obtain all the nutrients they need for their first few weeks from their mother's milk, which contains all the necessary nutrients. There are instances where a kitten's mother may not be around because of death, illness or when the mother rejects her kitten upon giving birth. In such instance, formulated commercial milk is always the best option. Unlike some breed of cats, the growth of Birman kittens is slow. The commercial milk you buy must therefore contain adequate amounts of all the nutrients in balanced quantities. It is important to point out that kittens do require energy three times that of adult cats and proteins two times that of adult cats.

Adult Cat Nutrition Needs

Meeting nutrition needs of an adult cat can be a serious challenge. Not only should an adult cat have enough to eat but also consume a diet rich in all the necessary nutrients. An adult Birman cat is not only active and therefore requires increased amount of energy; it also requires increased amounts of protein for repair of body tissues and for other body functions as well. It also requires increased amounts of essential fats, particularly during cold weather. Although it is very necessary that you feed your cat on these, you need to be careful so as not to make your cat obese. It is very important to note that although your adult cat will need the same amount of nutrients during adulthood, there are exceptions. Periods when your cat is sick or pregnant will definitely raise the need to buy food containing the amount of nutrients necessary, taking into account your cat's condition.

Old Cat Nutrition Needs

Just in the same way that feeding kittens and adult cats differ, feeding an old cat also differs. You are most likely to start noticing your Birman cat's aging signs when it is about fifteen years old. Because of body changes, metabolic and immunologic changes it is bound to go through, occurrence of such age-related diseases/health conditions as loss of muscle mass, arthritis, obesity and dental problems among others become common.

Taking into account the changes in an old cat's body and the likelihood of development of the indicated diseases/health conditions, a diet for an old cat should be one that promotes good health and appropriate body weight. Such a diet should ideally be low on carbohydrates but high on proteins, vitamins, essential fatty acids and minerals.

The Right Food

You have two options when it comes to the right food for your cat; canned and dry food, which at times is referred to as dry kibble. Compared to canned food, dry food stuffs have low water content, high on carbohydrates and plant protein. Considering that cats are carnivorous animals, dry kibble is not the right food for your cat.

Although your cat needs foods rich in protein, it is better off with animal-based protein. Feeding your cat plant-based protein derived from vegetables simply has no value to your cat in terms of nutrition. Unlike plant-based protein, animal-based protein contains amino acids, the essential fats that are beneficial to your cat. Canned food contains animal-based protein, making canned food the right food for your cat.

Although canned food cannot be said to be that fresh, dry kibble goes through a lot of processing in addition to being cooked at high temperatures for a long time. This does not only lower quality of protein within but also damages other nutrients.

The benefit of canned cat food over dry kibble is also in the amount of water contained. Cats generally do not drink water since their prey in the wild supplies them with enough amount of water. Having a cat at home therefore requires that you feed it on a diet rich in water, which makes canned food the right food for your cat.

You have two options when it comes to cat food. The first option is to prepare cat food on your own at home or the other option is to buy commercial canned foods. It is important to look at these two options to enable you make the right decision when it comes to food for your cat.

Unknown to some cat owners, cats are carnivorous animals and therefore rely on eating raw meat. Whether it is fresh or raw meat is neither here nor there since wild cats kill their prey and may not consume the whole prey in one instance. Cat owners who have a negative view on feeding their cats on raw meat therefore deny their cats what they are actually supposed to eat. A common belief by such cat owners usually has to do with the element of food poisoning.

Unlike us humans who are highly susceptible to food poisoning, cats are not. This is because while the food we eat resides in our intestines for anything between 35 and 55 hours, the food that a cat eats only resides in its intestine for between 12 and 16 hours. This simply means that any harmful bacteria remain within a cat's intestine for a short period of time unlike in humans. The short period of time therefore lowers the risk of food poisoning.

It is therefore perfectly in order to buy raw meat to feed your cat on. Even as you do so, you need to remember that not all raw meat sources are the same in quality. You need to consider buying whole cuts of meat that you can thoroughly clean before feeding your cat on instead of buying pre-ground meats available in supermarkets.

It can be very fulfilling if you opt to prepare for your cat its food at home. Even as you do so, it is very important that you do not subject your cat to the same meat source. You seriously need to consider changing meat sources. You have the option of feeding your cat on beef, rabbit meat or chicken among others. You also need to consider adding in some water and recommended supplements.

The second option is to go for commercial cat food and in this case canned cat foods. There is however a serious challenge you are likely to face when shopping for canned cat food; marketing gimmicks or food labels. Some of the food labels you are most likely to come across on canned cat foods include "For Indoor-Only Cat", "Natural", "Premium", "Breed Specific", Veterinarian Recommended" and "Therapeutic Diet" among other labels.

Although they seem very promising, some of the food labels can be very misleading. The reality is that most canned foods with these labels contain wheat, corn, soy and by-products. While wheat, corn and soy definitely have high levels of carbohydrate that your cat does not really need, the by-products happen to be the only source of protein for your cat, which is not appropriate.

The only effective way to overcome the challenge presented by promising yet false food labels is to look at both the composition and ingredients used in making canned cat food when shopping. While the composition part of it refers to percentage of fat, protein and carbohydrate cat food contains, ingredients refer to the specific nutrients in the food. You need to pay attention to three important things when it comes to choosing the right canned cat food; it should food be food that is high in water content, low in carbohydrates and contain animal-based protein instead of plant-based protein.

It is worth pointing out that mainstream canned cat foods can at times be very expensive, depending on your location. This is because they do contain muscle meat of chicken and turkey among others, which is normally listed as the first ingredient. Depending on your financial position, you may consider buying canned cat foods that contains by-products. These are normally labeled as "chicken by-products" or "turkey by-products" among others. The fact that they are affordable does not mean that they are of no nutrition value.

Like with all canned foods, canned cat foods do feature preservatives and ascertaining the kind of preservative used in cat food is very important. There are canned cat foods that contain such preservatives as ethoxyguin, BHA and BHT. These are chemicals that have been proved not to be safe when used as preservatives. Although most cat food manufacturers have abandoned the use of such preservatives, you need to check to ensure that canned cat food you are about to buy does not contain the same.

Feeding Program

There is really no uniform cat feeding program. This is the frequency at which you need to feed your cat. How frequently you feed your Birman kitten, adult cat or an old cat definitely differs. This is because they need to feed at different intervals and in different amounts at every stage of their life. Your home environment and type of food you feed your cat on also informs feeding frequency.

Just like with human babies, kittens need to be fed small amounts of food at regular intervals. This is because their tummies are not yet capable of handling large amounts of food yet this is the time they need sufficient amount of various nutrients necessary for growth and development. Birman kittens generally need to be fed at least four meals spread out in any given day.

Unlike kittens that need to eat nutritious food for growth and development, your adult Birman cat needs to eat maintenance food. This is food that does not only aid in further development of the body but in maintaining strong healthy bones and in enhancing the body's immune system. Because it can be difficult to ascertain the amount of food that your adult cat needs, it is better to let it eat until it is satisfied. Two meals in any given day should be enough.

Just in the same way that feeding kittens differs from feeding adult cats, feeding an old Birman cat also differs. Old cats are generally susceptible to various diseases and health conditions that make it necessary to tailor their feeding frequency taking into account any health problems they may have. The same goes for sick kittens and adult cats.

It is important to look at the feeding program for adult cats because such is the cat you are most likely to have. You have two options when it comes to designing a feeding program for your cat. Your first option is to let your cat get used to a free feeding program, where you fill its feeding dish with large amount of food that it can eat when it wishes. Although this program best suits a cat that is often left alone at home for a considerable amount of time, it has its disadvantages. First, you are obligated to buy kibble cat food because fresh food may not last long in the open. Secondly, there is the risk of your cat over-eating and therefore developing obesity.

Your other option is to design a scheduled feeding program where your cat gets used to a specific time when it is served food. This program can be very beneficial considering the fact that you are literally in a position to control how much food your cat consumes at any given time.

The fact that you have designed a feeding program for your cat should not mean that such a program is permanent. There is always room to alter a program depending on different situations such as when travelling, when your cat is sick, when your cat is pregnant (if a female and not spayed) and when adverse weather changes occur.

Food Allergies

Just like it is with humans, cats too develop different allergies including inhalant, flea bite and food allergies. In the case of food, cats generally develop food allergies when subjected to specific food stuff on a regular basis. Birman cats do develop allergies when they are between two and six years although a few have been noted to develop food allergy as early as when they are five months old and when they are as old as fifteen years old.

Contrary to popular belief, food allergy does not necessarily mean food intolerance. Unlike food intolerance that manifests itself in the form of diarrhea and/or vomiting, food allergy exhibits real symptoms that may include itchy skin, hair loss and excessive scratching among other symptoms.

Causes of food allergy in cats are usually specific ingredients found in cat foods and in particular in such cat food stuffs as corn, soy, dairy products, wheat and seafood. It is worth noting that these are the same food stuffs found in dry or kibble cat foods.

Determining whether or not your cat suffers from food allergy can be a very big challenge. This is because food allergy symptoms are in most cases similar to those presented by such cat diseases/health conditions as flea bite allergy and intestinal parasite hypersensitivity. However, there are several ways through which you can determine whether or not your cat suffers from food allergy or other diseases, although determination can take some time.

The most effective way through which you can determine whether or not your cat suffers from food allergy is to undertake food trials. This means subjecting your cat to a specific type of food for several days while looking out for any allergy symptoms. It is important to note that blood tests are only effective in diagnosing other types of allergies but not food allergy.

There are instances where your cat's food allergy and associated symptoms become serious. This is usually the time to take your cat to a vet for examination and treatment. Your vet will most likely feed your cat fatty acids, steroids and prescribe antihistamines as the first line of treatment. The only effective way of treating food allergy in cats is avoidance of causative food.

What Not to Feed Your Cat

Food that is edible to you and/or your dog may not be edible to your cat. Feeding your cat on certain food stuffs cannot only cause allergies and intoxication, consumption of certain food stuffs can easily lead to your cat going into coma with increased risk of instant death. It is perfectly normal to have alcoholic beverages at home so long as you keep them safe and away from your cat. Your cat will definitely be intoxicated when it consumes any food containing alcohol and can easily go into coma with high chances of dying.

Spices make food very tasty but only to humans. Feeding your cat on spices can cause serious allergic reaction and toxicity, which can lead to death. Cats are carnivorous animals and therefore do well with meat but not bones. Whether from fish, beef, lamb or poultry, bones are simply dangerous to your cat. Not only can they cause obstruction; bones can also lacerate your cat's digestive system and cause serious problems.

You should not feed or let your cat feed on such food stuffs as tea, chocolate, coffee and caffeine. These contain caffeine, theophylline and theobromine. These are ingredients that cause vomiting and other health problems in cats.

While both human vitamin and mineral supplements can indeed be healthy, they can be very dangerous when you feed your cat on them. You need to keep all your food supplements far from reach of your cat. These are just a few of food stuffs that you should not feed your cat on. Although your cat will naturally avoid some of these food stuffs, you need to safely keep away those that it can accidentally consume.

Cat Treats

Giving your cat treats occasionally is highly recommended. Contrary to common belief by some cat owners, cat treats are not entirely valueless. Modern cat treats are formulated to encourage good dental, digestive, general and skin health, depending on type of treat you buy. Note that there are crunchy, dental, soft, catnip/grass and jerky cat treats. You also have the option of buying grain-free, natural or organic cat treats. To enhance their appeal and taste, cat treats are in most cases flavored. You may choose to buy beef, chicken, vegetarian, turkey, tuna or fish flavored treats.

Your cat definitely needs intake of calories that cat treats provide. However, it is very important that you measure the amount of treats you feed your cat. Because cat treats largely contain calories, they should not make up more than 10% of your cat's calorie intake. Your cat should obtain the remaining 90% from quality nutritious foods.

Like with shopping for canned cat food, it is important that you choose cat treats with utmost care. This is because some information contained on cat treat labels may not be correct. You seriously need to look out for the amount of calories a cat treat food contains before you buy it.

When to feed your cat treats is very important. This is because there is increased risk of your cat developing addiction or taste for treats instead of its regular foods. Because of this, you need to feed your cat treats at special occasions only. Such can be when it does something positive like mastering a rule and excelling in an exercise or training.

Because cat treats basically contain calories, they are not recommended for overweight cats. Feeding your overweight cat treats will simply worsen its condition and increase the risk of serious health conditions. For an overweight cat, go for Catnip/grass treats. Both are cereal grasses and therefore low on calories.

You should be able to find different types of cat treats on the market. There are those that are soft and moist and those that are hard, just similar to dry cat food. Your cat will most likely hate dry treats and be in favor of soft treats. It is always a good idea to balance between the two for your cat to receive all the nutrients it needs for good health.

There are a number of cat treat brands in the market and just like with choosing canned food carefully, you need to choose cat treats carefully. The most important things to look into are the ingredients a treat is composed of. This is very necessary because some cat treats may contain ingredients that may cause allergies.

How you store cat treats you buy is of great importance. The Birman is a very clever cat and will notice when you feed it on treats. It will therefore look for the same where you store its canned food. It may develop the habit of stealing treats if you fail to store the same in a secure place. The best way to go about storing cat treats is to store the same in a different location from where you store its regular food.

Chapter Five: Grooming Your Birman Cat

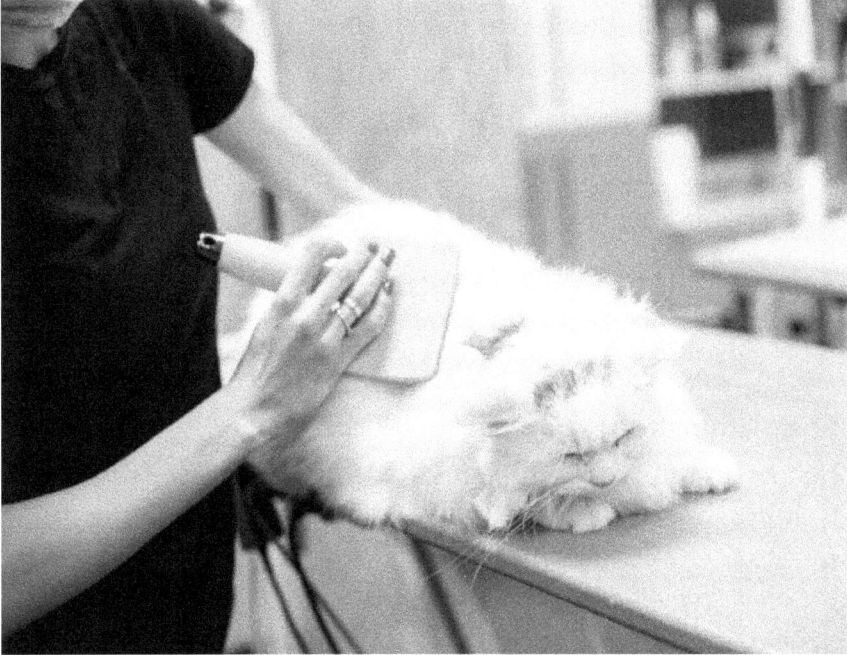

Daily grooming is necessary for the long-haired breeds like Birman cats. If they are left neglected and uncombed, it will result into matting of hair. These will be so deep and tight to the skin that shaving will be the only option left.

The long hair should be brushed against the direction of hair, i.e., from the tail towards the head. For this purpose, a brush, which has bristles in rows in a half-moon shaped head should be used. Always brush in upward and forward direction. The hair tangles should be removed gently and then coat can be brushed. A toothbrush can be used for the fine hair of face.

While grooming one can check cat's general body, condition, i.e. eyes, ears, mouth and claws. Eyes should be wiped with cotton wool dipped in lukewarm water and a separate cotton swab should be used for each eye. Persian cat's eyes should be cleaned properly as their snub nose interfere with functioning of tear ducts which results into weepy eyes.

Ears

These should be examined for dirt, excess wax, mites or inflammation. The wax should be cleaned with a pad or bud of cotton wool moistened with warm water or baby oil. It should be done carefully to avoid damage to the delicate lining of ear.

Teeth

Birman cats should be fed with such type of food which provides enough exercise and cleaning of teeth and gums. Mostly cats are given minced fine diet, which they swallow at a gulp and may result in choking and as there is nothing to chew, it often results in dental tartar and other tooth problems.

Birman cats, which have outdoors activity, are less prone to such problems as they may catch and eat prey and have chance to clean, exercise and strengthen the teeth. Thus, to avoid such problems in indoor cats, they should be fed with solid meat i.e., beef skin or skinned hind leg of a rabbit at least every two weeks or so. Along with this dry cat foods are also helpful in preventing the tartar. All these are applicable to cats having a normal jaw structure while long-haired breeds having short faces need regular attention by the vet and owner to keep clean teeth. Scaling of tartar is not the solution of this problem as it may lead to inflammation of gums. So, it is advisable to check the teeth during grooming to control any related problem in the initial stages.

Claws

Birman cats getting adequate scratching facilities rarely need to have their claws clipped, but they should be checked while grooming to ensure that the nails are not overgrown. There are various types of nail clippers available for pets, but the clippers which slip over the claw can result in injury if the animal is struggling. So, clippers should be used cautiously and the trimming must be done with great care. Claws can be retracted by gently pressing the paw and the plain horn tip beyond the quick (a pinkish color) can be seen. The cut should be made along the base of the nail and quick should not be cut as it will be very painful and cat may fight against any attempt to treat the feet. So, only the tips should be clipped and not the sensitive 'quick'.

Bathing

Normally a cat should not be bathed. If it is done forcefully, the cat will become frightened and this may destroy the relationship of mutual trust between the owner and the cat. Sometimes there is no other alternative except bathing a cat if its coat is soiled with paint or tar, which cannot be removed with petrol or other cleaning agents as they may burn their skin.

For bathing, care should be taken to complete it fast and efficiently, just to prevent unnecessary stress. The basin should be large enough and fitted with rubber mat to prevent slipping. It should be on table as two people can work together, i.e., one can hold and console the cat, While other can give bath to cat. The water should be warm enough and cat shampoo should be used. However, baby shampoo can also be used. Never use dog or other shampoo, which might contain elements harmful for cat's skin.

The cat should be wet thoroughly and then shampoo should be applied to make lather, then rinse the coat with clean warm water so as to remove the shampoo from fur. Head should be washed only if necessary and care should be taken to avoid eyes and ears. After bathing, the cat should be wrapped in towel and should be dried gently when the coat is completely dry, only then it should be placed in warm place because cat may subject to chill as it has been soaked to the skin. If frequent bathing is required then it is better to use a dry method of cleaning the coat. For this purpose, a bran, warm enough up to cat's skin temperature should be rubbed into the coat, leaving it for a while and then brushing it out along with dirt and grease, to leave the fur shining and clean. A cat occasionally tends to produce excess natural oil at base of tail to make that area greasy. This is most often seen in male cats and is known as 'stud tail' and can be cleaned by the bran method. This method is good for short-haired cats while long-haired cats can be dry shampooed using talcum powder, i.e., rubbed in and brushed out as is done for bran. Long hair should be combed to remove knots and matts as they may tangle in process of rubbing, bathing or dry treatment.

Chapter Six: Raising and Training a Birman Cat

How To Train Cats?

Cats are brilliant animals, and no matter how old they are, they can learn to behave well. Like any other type of upbringing, a cat's education must be based on support, rewarding good behavior, and pointing to the undesirable.

Maybe your Birman cat already knows to behave well when she comes to live with your family, but educating a cat is a process that never stops. A cat can quickly adopt bad habits, as well, and then it takes time until the issues are solved, mostly if you tolerate such behavior for a while. However, bad behavior can be prevented with the right response - while training the cat, encouraging it for good behavior, and never mind when it misbehaves. Your kitten will quickly connect praise and reward with the right actions and forget about the behavior you ignore.

When thinking about education, think about what you expect your cat to do, why would you want it to do that, and when will you will reward them. Cats are motivated mainly by food, but unfortunately, this only works when they are hungry! However, it is good to find a treat that your cat particularly enjoys, which will help their upbringing. Educating and disciplining cats is different from disciplining a dog, so you will not ask your cat to respond to commands such as "sit" or similar. However, you can teach your cat to respect some parts of your home so that, for example, they knew that they could not scratch furniture.

Cats are naturally clean animals and are looking for a litter box to defecate. Check the box every time to see if it is not accidentally moved. The litter box should be in a quiet place, away from food containers, easily accessible and clean. If your cat is upset and seeks other sites for defecation, you need to change the box's position. The cat will quickly return to the habit of using the box, now when it's in the new place.

The following techniques tips and tricks cover a variety of situations that most cat owners encounter. First, in dressage, think about what you want to teach the Birman cat to specify that this is done most effectively. The crucial part of cat training is consistency. No matter what you choose, make sure that you do it regularly; otherwise, you will be sending your cat mixed signals, which will further aggravate its development. Do not think that cat training finishes in 10 minutes.

Remember these tips to make your Birman cat training easier:

1. Punishment means nothing to cats!

It is a fact! If you ever had a dog, you know that punishing him will help change their behavior. It does not bide well with cats. Do not waste your time - they will just sit there purring and then continue with the same action.

2. Corporal punishment is not an option.

Because the cat's body is so gentle, do not hit the cat. This means that you must use other methods to outwit and achieve what you want when training your cat. We do not doubt that you will succeed in doing so.

3. Use a form of positive reinforcement.

As you become a cat owner, you will find it difficult to "catch the cat in action" (preferably a wrongdoing). Therefore, it is much easier to reward your cat when you see good behavior. Ensure you have cat treats for your cat every time it does something useful, such as using the sandbox.

4. Get plenty of toys.

You can buy them at the store for pets or make them yourself. Cats are habitually naughty because they are bored. They are by nature predators. Remember the scene from the animated film "The Lion King" when small Samba learns lessons of stalking prey. When your cat goes down on the curtains and runs towards the wall, they're just practicing their predatory skills. Provide the cat with sufficient alternative materials to practice.

5. Make sure that the cat is "fun while you're gone."

If your cat is used to society, it will quickly become bored with solitude and slowly begin to destroy things while you are at work or no one at home for a long time.

6. Learn the value of the spray bottle of water.

In some cases, spraying a cat with water is sufficient to get their attention and stop the bad behavior. All you need is a sprayer that you usually use to spray houseplants. When the cat starts to misbehave, you squirt. Soon, they'll know what is allowed and what not.

7. Blow in your cat's face.

It may sound strange, but it works. If your cat comes centimeters from your face and you want to teach it to keep a certain distance and give you some space, try this trick - simply blow into her face. The cat will startle and puzzle. Soon they will realize that they should not bother you anymore.

8. Make sure your cat has a room with a view.

You know the saying "curiosity killed the cat." It happens that the owner is angry because of something the cat has done, because of boredom. Many feline negative behaviors are associated with their curiosity. Ensure that your cat can sit on the windowsill and watch the birds flying outside or whatever's happening up there. If your windowsill is not big enough for the cat to sit there longer, try to expand the board.

9. Deal with the cat.

This might sound strange as a training technique, but the more time you spend with your cat, the better you will be able to communicate with them. Cats have well-developed communication skills. The better you know your cat, and the better it knows you; it will be easier for you to read their thoughts. A lot easier for you to understand what the cat is about to do. This goes both ways–the cat will know when you disagree with what it does by learning your body language.

10. You have more than one cat?

Cats will always fight over territory. If a fight starts while you are in the vicinity, the first thing you do is stop it. The best technique is spraying water over the cats. Spray the aggressor, and avoid spreading the victim cat. After that, close the aggressor cat in another room. During this time, reward the cat who did not react, even though it was attacked.

These ideas are just a small part of the cat's upbringing. When you become more familiar with your cat, you will develop your communication. This can be done through speech - you're talking to it, and she mews, but the body's language is what matters the most. Soon you will discern the nuances of this form of communication, and raising the cats will be easier than you thought.

The Difference between Training an Older Birman Cat and a Kitten

Age does not matter to cat lovers. If they want to take a Birman cat in their house, old or young will do. However, how do they manage? If learning is possible with older humans, it is also possible with older cats. We only need extra patience for older cats, just like you would for older humans.

We know kittens are more comfortable to train because they are like clean slates that you can write on without erasing anything. It is acceptable if they fail or make accidents because they are young and do not understand many things yet. You will have to deal with their teeth and claws, which are very sharp. Yikes!

Older cats may make you go excited, especially if you see one in the adoption and you know that it is the right cat for you. It can also make you a skeptic because it may have been through training already. There's also the chance that it didn't go through any training and it will be difficult for you. People think that if trying to teach a person to unlearn the bad things he has learned before is hard, what more to a cat who does not even know how to speak?

Still, do not let it hold you back. First, older cats are less aggressive unless they have been abused, injured, and given a hard time. If the cat you are planning to adopt has been through a hard time, you need tons of patience and understanding.

Like any abused creature, cats will become defensive, and they will respond either by running away from you quickly or hiss and trying to scratch you. Cats that have undergone hardship need an understanding owner to help them. You have to enable it to interact generally with people and other animals first before starting the behavior training.

It is challenging but very rewarding once your cat is back to normal.

For normal yet older cats, you still need patience but not as much. Since you do not have any problems interacting with other creatures, you can start by helping them familiarize themselves with their new surroundings first. Remember, cats know when their environment has changed. Let it grow comfortable a bit and start training it with the essential behavior depending on how it already behaves as soon as it is comfortable in its new home.

If you notice your new cat uses every spot of your home as a toilet, address that first and train it for housebreaking. If it has a habit of chewing or scratching essential or dangerous things in the house like electrical cords, address that first as it is more critical than housebreaking.

Take note of your Birman cat's attitude first before starting to train it. Chances are, on its first arrival in your home, it will seem well-behaved and scared. Its right behavior will show as soon as it feels comfortable already.

Birman cats can even learn tricks, but it is always important to finish and polish a specific training before moving on to another. Do not train your cat or kitten with several behaviors or skills simultaneously because this will only cause him confusion and anxiety.

The Basics Of Training

Dogs get all the training glory, but cats can be trained, too! You just have to understand what motivates their behavior. Many cat owners feel as if they are on their own when it comes to training because there are no cat behavior consultants in their area, but many behavior consultants and trainers offer virtual consultations. If you are having trouble, you can reach out to them via phone, Facetime, Skype, or Zoom.

The important thing to remember about cat training is that it is a huge lesson in positive reinforcement training, because cats don't respond to negative punishments. Positive reinforcement training means taking opportunities to reward the behavior you want and offering the cat better alternative choices for behavior you do not want.

Below you'll find detailed steps about how to do various types of training, including clicker training.

Clicker Training

Most dog people have heard of clicker training, but cats also respond to this style of training quite well. In fact, I have found anecdotally that cats respond to clicker training very quickly if good things happen when they hear the clicker. When you say positive words like "good girl," your tone or inflection can give the cat mixed signals; also, these words may be used in various situations that fail to provide a reinforcer like a treat. A clicker is more consistent.

There are two types of clicker training: operant training and classical training. Let's look at these two techniques a bit more closely, and then I will give you some lessons to help you learn how to use the clicker to change your cat's behavior.

Operant training is opportunity training. The cat presents you with a desired behavior, and you have the opportunity to reinforce the behavior. Classical training, also called classical conditioning, is much like Pavlov's dogs who learned to drool every time the bell rang. Classical conditioning depends on a natural reflexive response to a stimulus.

Using a clicker in training is a form of two-way communication with your cat. You and your cat learn what to expect from each other in a way that is fun for both of you and naturally reinforces the bond between you. Not only will your cat learn something new, you will feel less frustrated and the environment in the home will be happier for everyone.

Be sure that the rewards you give for positive behavior are of sufficient value to your cat. Your clicker is a conditioning tool and the high-value reward is the reinforcer.

One last thing about clicker training: Some cats are frightened by the loud sound of dog clickers. If that is the case with your cat, you can use a tool called a soft clicker, a pen that clicks when you open or close it, or even a tongue knock. Whatever tool you choose needs to be easy for you to use consistently.

Practice Using The Clicker

In this lesson you'll learn how to use the clicker. This lesson may seem silly at first glance, but it is important that you get comfortable with the tool. Clicker training is about watching for the desired behavior, clicking when the cat exhibits the behavior, and rapidly rewarding the behavior. If you fumble with the clicker or the treat, you will give the cat mixed messages.

To Practice Using The Clicker, You Will Need:

- Clicker
- Treat bag or container
- Treats
- Full length mirror or the ability to record yourself on your phone

Steps:

1. Practice holding the clicker and clicking. Try it in both hands, because during training you will use one hand to click and the other to deliver a reward rapidly.
2. Practice holding the clicker as still as possible. I like to hold the clicker behind my back, but you might like it at your side or waist. The point is to keep the body still during the click.

3. Practice clicking and at the same time placing a treat on the floor in front of you. If you keep fumbling your treat bag or container, consider changing to one that is easier for you.

4. Once you think you have the actions down, watch yourself in the mirror or record yourself doing a rapid click/reward 10 times in succession. Look for excess body movements and any fumbling with the clicker or treats. Continue to work on your skills until you have improved so they are not distracting.

Charging The Clicker And Your Cat

You can use the clicker in classical conditioning to help your cat make the association between the clicker and the reward. This entire lesson shouldn't take more than two to three minutes to complete. Practice this twice a day.

Things You Will Need For This Exercise:

- Clicker
- High-value treat
- Quiet room

Steps:

1. Place your cat in the quiet room or area.
2. Sit or stand in front of your cat and click and deliver treats in rapid succession. As soon as your cat finishes one treat, click and provide another.

3. Watch for your cat to start looking for the click or at you. Click and reward when this behavior begins. You have moved from classical conditioning to operant training, and your cat is ready to offer you opportunities to reward behaviors.

4. Put the treats and clicker away. You are done with the lesson.

Come When Called

This valuable lesson is one that can get your cat out of danger, help find them if they dart out the door, and locate them if they are hiding. Most cats will already show up when they hear the treat bag rustle, so what we are really doing is putting that behavior on a cue so we can use the clicker in other circumstances. Keep the training sessions short. About five minutes twice a day is enough.

Things You Will Need For This Exercise:

- Clicker
- High-value treats
- Quiet room

Steps:

1. Place your cat in a quiet area.
2. Provide two or three clicks and rewards to charge the session.
3. Move away from your cat.

4. When your cat begins to walk toward you, say your cat's name, click, and give them a treat.
5. Once your cat is responding well in the quiet room, start practicing in other areas around the home that have more distractions.
6. Eventually, replace the treats with head scratches and cheek rubs.

Targeting

Teaching your cat a targeting behavior helps you shape other behaviors—such as leading them to their cat tree, a veterinary exam table, or other locations.

For targeting training, you can use a target stick with a built-in clicker, your finger, or a simple tool—I have even used a wooden spoon or Popsicle stick. Practice the steps below for a few minutes several times a day.

Things You Will Need For This Exercise:

- Clicker
- High-value treats
- Target stick or other tool

Steps:

1. Place your Birman cat in front of you.
2. Offer the target to your cat.
3. When your cat moves to sniff the target, click and reward.

4. Once your cat is consistently moving toward the target or touching it with their nose, start offering the target in different positions.
5. Move farther away from your cat. When they start to move toward the target, click and reward, using the verbal cue "target."
6. Continue to create distance between your cat and the target, clicking and rewarding your cat when they move toward the target.
7. Make a slow circle around your cat, offering the target and pausing to click and reward them as they turn toward the target. Put this behavior on cue by saying "spin."

Go To Box/Mat

Go to box is useful if you need your cat to go to a certain location and stay there. You will use this exercise for all your departures or arrivals home. This is an excellent exercise if you have a door dasher! The box type I recommend is the canned cat food tray from a case of cat food, which you can get for free from any pet food supply store. You can also use a small towel, mat, or cat bed.

Things You Will Need For This Exercise:

- Clicker
- High-value treat
- Box (or other place for the cat to lie down)

Steps:

1. Call your cat to come to you. Click and reward.
2. Place the box on the floor between you and your cat.
3. Let your cat sniff the box. Click and reward.
4. If your cat puts one paw in the box, click and reward by tossing the treat outside the box. You may be tempted to lure them into the box, but at this point you want your cat to offer the behavior and give you the opportunity to reward them. You can also use your target stick to get this behavior started by having them target in the box.
5. Once your cat is successfully putting one paw in the box, wait to click until they have two front paws in the box. Then click and reward.
6. Continue building on this exercise until your cat is fully sitting in the box.
7. Create some distance between you and the box and cue your cat to "go to box." Once your cat is in the box, wait a few seconds and then click and reward by tossing the treats away from the box. Start with a few seconds. Gradually increase the time they need to wait, with the goal of getting them to wait for a few minutes.
8. Move the box to other locations around your home and ask your cat to "go to box." Have them wait in the box and then click and toss treats away from the box.
9. Once your cat knows to "go to box," use this behavior to be able to walk out the door without the cat dashing

to get through. For example, you can ask your cat to go to box, wait, place rewards on the floor, and then click as you walk out the door.

10. When returning, immediately ask your cat to "go to box" and click/reward. It will take some time, but your cat will learn that good things happen if they stay in the box when you come and go, rather than darting out the door.

Come Along

Once your cat has mastered targeting behavior, use it to teach them to "come along." This behavior is helpful when you need your cat to come with you to a certain location. The come along exercise builds trust between you and your cat by teaching them that you won't take them anywhere dangerous. You can use it when you do harness training to walk your cat outside or to bring the cat back if they should dart out the door.

Things You Will Need For This Exercise:

- Clicker
- High-value treats
- Target stick

Steps:

1. Call your cat to come to you. Click and reward.
2. Hold the target at your side at about knee height and say "target." Click and reward.

3. Turn your back to your cat and take three steps away from them, with the target remaining at your knee. Say "target." Click and reward. Take three more steps away and repeat. Continue until the cat is following you.

4. Repeat step 3, changing the cue word to "come along" or "follow." Have your cat come along with you to different locations in the house.

Up/Down

Teaching your cat up and down is both useful and fun. When used to address counter surfing, your cat will learn that that the countertop is a no reward zone. Conversely, they learn where they can go up, like the sofa, your lap, or the windowsill. Remember that when you discourage one behavior like leaping onto the countertop, you need to replace it with an alternative behavior.

Things You Will Need For This Exercise:

- Clicker
- High-value treats
- Cat tree
- Target stick

Steps:

1. Start slow and work with a low cat tree first. Using your target stick, say "target" while pointing at the top of the cat tree. Click and reward, using the cue "up."

Some cats enjoy the "up" and they will perform it just to receive attention from you. Practice "up" until your cat does it on cue.

2. Hold your target stick on the floor and cue the word "down." If the cat jumps down, click and reward.

3. Once the cat responds to the up/down cues at the cat tree, add a third location and practice cueing your cat to go up, down, and up again. When the cat responds to the cue, click and reward.

4. We want to ignore the unwanted behavior of surfing for attention and have the cat get down and then go to the third location. This might be a barstool or low cat tree in the kitchen, where they can observe and not be in the way. Some people have their cats actually go up on top of the cabinets as their alternative location. You might decide "go to box" on a corner of the counter works as well.

Sit Pretty

Building on some of the skills you have already learned, you can teach your cat to Sit Pretty. This little show-off trick is fun.

Things You Will Need For This Exercise:

- Clicker
- High-value Treats
- Target stick

Steps:

1. Call your cat to come to you. Click and reward.
2. Wait for the cat to sit on its own. Click and reward by tossing the treat away from you.
3. Call the cat again. When they come back to you, wait for the cat to sit, then cue the word "sit." Click and reward, again by tossing the treat away from you.
4. Once your cat is sitting consistently, hold your target stick high over their head. Your cat should sit up or start to reach up to the target. Click and reward. Start using the cue "sit pretty."
5. Once your cat is consistently sitting or sitting pretty, fade the use of the clicker and reward.
6. Sit and Sit Pretty can be tedious tricks to learn, so keep sessions brief. Practice several times a day.

High Five

This is another fun trick for you and your cat. It is generally easy to teach.

Things You Will Need For This Exercise:

- Clicker
- High-value treats

Steps:

1. Sit on the floor in front of your cat with a treat in your closed fist. Hold your fist out at the height of the cat's shoulder.
2. When your cat puts their paw on your fist, click and give the treat.
3. Repeat several times until your cat consistently puts their paw on your fist when you hold it out.
4. If your cat doesn't reach with their paw for the treat, start with your fist at floor level and let them paw at your hand. Gradually work up to the cat's shoulder level.
5. When your cat responds consistently, start offering your hand palm up without the treat.
6. Click and reward with your other hand when your cat puts their paw in your hand.

Toilet Training

This training is very, very important. Like potty training your puppy, getting your kitten to be potty trained is one of the most useful things you can teach her. But this doesn't come too easy. It'll take some time and efforts. Why should you potty train your kitten? The next sub-header highlights the two major benefits.

Why you should train your kitten to use the toilet

- You'll enjoy a cleaner home

- Your kitten learns to be self-coordinated
-

How To Train Your Kitten To Use The Toilet

Start the training on time

Getting your kitten to learn to use the toiled requires that you start immediately he's around 12 to 16 weeks old. At this stage, his bladder is developed enough for him to be able to hold urine.

Confine her to a small area

During this period, you should ensure that your kitten is confined to a particular area. It could be her crate. This will help prevent her from messing up the house when no one is around.

Watch out for toilet signs

Normally, your kitten will give signs that she needs to go out to attend to nature's call. Watch out for signs like pacing, scratching, or sniffing around. When you notice these signs, just take her out so she can do her business.

Place a litter box near your toilet

First, put a litter box adjacent to your toilet. Afterward gradually bring it closer and closer to the top of the seat- you might place a stool to make this easy for your cat. When she's used to using a litter box on top of the toilet, change to a special litter box that fits within the toilet. When she's used to climbing the toilet, gradually use less and less litter so that she gets used to ding her business without it. Thereafter, remove the litter box entirely.

Alternatively, you can follow the under listed steps:

- Place your kitten beside a neat litter box, in a confined area, like a room in your house (ensure your kitten has enough food and clean water).
- Immediately your kitten has finished eaten, place her in the litter box.
- Normally, after three or four days of being confined with the box, she'd get used to doing her business in the box.

Create a schedule

During this learning stage, you'd need to take your kitten out regularly. Take her out first thing in the morning and every one hour throughout the day. Take her out after she has eaten or woken from a nap. Do not forget to take her out before she goes to bed. And when you're taking her out, please do not take her to different toilet locations. Take her to same place every time. It could be her personal toilet. This will send a lasting message to her brain. It's like you're telling her,

'This is where you should do your business.' Whenever she's pressed, you can be sure she'd go to the same location.

Praise your kitten

Whenever your kitten goes to the toilet herself to do her business, please do not hesitate to give her lots of praises. You could say something like, 'oh dear, you're so lovely,' while you smile and pat her forehead. This will motivate her to want to please you more or be responsive to other trainings. Apart from praising your kitten, you can use treats. Giving her a piece of cake or taking her out to catch some fun will also create a positive impression on her.

It is good to keep in mind that getting your cat to be trained to use the toilet isn't a one-day easy affair. It comes with challenges. Let us see a few of those challenges.

Challenges of training your kitten to use the toilet

It can be really frustrating to keep teaching your kitten not to do her business in the living room or in the kitchen or in any really awkward places around your home, but she isn't responsive. You might even be tempted to raise your voice at her or raise a club to threaten her. But please do not, like toddlers, kittens are easily scared and mild hearted. You would only be making them run from you.

Some of the things that can make getting your kitten to use the toilet a bit difficult include;

- All kittens aren't the same. Some kittens are slow learners and may get you to be fed up. But do not worry; they'd get over it soon. Be patient with your kitten.
- Like puppies some kittens are very stubborn. One kitten I raised in 2016 was just frustrating and unyielding. No matter how often I took her out, she still preferred my sofa for her business. Well, I decided to add a bit of aggression. So, each time she messed up my sofa, I'd scold and whip her a little until finally she got to understand that messing up my living room made me angry.

Common Cat Behaviors

When becoming a first-time cat owner, there are 7 main cat behaviors you should be aware of. Recognizing these behaviors will help you communicate better with your cat and create a stronger bond between you. Let's review the 7 most common cat behaviors, so you will know what to do, and what not to do.

Twitching Tail

A wagging tail does not inevitably mean your cat is happy like it would if a dog were wagging its tail. A calm cat will slowly move its tail from side to side, while an anxious cat may move it in a quick jerking motion. If you see this, your cat is likely annoyed, and you should leave them alone. It also needs mentioning, but pulling your cat's tail is like someone pulling your hair. You wouldn't like it very much, and neither does your cat. Never pull your cat's tail.

Kneading

One of the strangest behaviors that new cat owners are surprised by is a behavior known as "kneading" or "kneading biscuits." This is something that came as a surprise to me, as I certainly had never heard of this before we had our second cat; and our first cat never did it.

"Kneading" is when you find your cat pushing down on a soft object, like a cushion or blanket, with their front paws and moving them back and forth in a rhythmic motion. It looks for all the world as if they are "kneading" some dough, ready to bake some bread or make a batch of cookies. They will usually be sitting up as they do so, but with a younger kitten, you may find they also have their face down "suckling" on the blanket as they knead.

This strange behavior is just your cat regressing to their early childhood, reliving the days of their younger selves when they were part of a litter, nursing on their mother. You will usually find that they are lightly purring while they do this and that they might fall off to sleep afterward.

It is the cat equivalent of a human child sucking their thumb, reminding themselves of the comfort of breastfeeding. The suckling action is easy to understand, but why the kneading? Well, when a kitten is breastfeeding, it uses its front paws to gently massage its mother's tummy to encourage the milk to flow freely. That action reminds them of nursing as much as the suckling does.

When your cat is kneading, it indicates that they are feeling very safe, secure, and content and are demonstrating that by settling down for a cozy relaxation session. If your cat comes and sits on you and starts purring and kneading in your lap, you should feel honored that they feel so relaxed and comfortable with you. They are letting you know that you make them feel as safe and secure as they did with their own mother. What a compliment!

Purring

While purring is usually a sign that your cat is happy, cats also purr when they are scared, anxious, in pain, or injured. While scientists don't have an answer as to why cats make the same sound in vastly different situations, they have made some guesses. A cat's purr has a frequency between 25 and 150 Hertz, which is the same frequency that has been found to promote the healing of bone and muscle. The conclusion is that cats purr to help their own bodies heal or to calm themselves. They can also help their humans or fellow feline friends heal by lying next to them while purring. I like to think of it as evolutionary purr-fection!

Burying and Scratching

A new cat owner may be perplexed while observing their kitty "burying" their food, or pawing around the bowl, after a meal. Cats in the wild bury the carcass of their kill so that it does not attract other threats. They may also be saving it for later, ensuring that it does not get eaten! Your kitty may also do the same thing after using its litter box, inside and even outside the litter box. This is because they are attempting to cover their smell to disguise it from predators. There may not be any predators in your home, but cats are driven by their instincts. Cats don't have a fridge to store food or the luxury of flushing their waste to hide it like us humans do, so they make do with what they can.

Exposing Their Belly

If your cat rolls over and exposes its belly to you, that means they trust you and are comfortable with you! It also generally means they want your attention. They may or may not let you rub their belly, but you will know their decision once you reach out to touch the fuzziness. This is your cat telling you to "Enjoy the cuteness, hooman!"

Vocalization

Cats meow solely to communicate with people, and not with each other. Cats meow to say hello, get our attention, ask for food or water, or when they want us to play with them. If you give them what they want, they will continue with this behavior. If you have fulfilled all their needs, and the meows continue, your cat may just be seeking attention. You can ignore your kitty's meows and they will learn that meowing will not always get them what they want and they will stop. However, if your furry friend is meowing excessively, it could be due to a medical problem and you should take your cat to a veterinarian to check if they are okay. An important note on this is that you should never hit or yell at your cat, as this will not make them quiet. Hitting and yelling will just make them afraid of you, and you don't want to verbally or physically abuse your pet. Foster a healthy and strong relationship with your little kitten and they will respond in kind.

Night Activity

Cats are known to be nocturnal creatures, but this is not completely accurate. There are two times of day where you will see the most activity from your cat: dawn and dusk. It is natural for cats to be active at night; this is because it is the prime time that rodents come out. However, they do not sleep all day and stay up all night. Your cat will take naps throughout the day and night. They have the instinct to hunt at nighttime, so it is a good idea to play with them during this time to reduce activity when you are trying to go to sleep. The "midnight crazies" may also be a sign that your kitty doesn't get enough playtime during the day. Try to spend a little more time with them or introduce new toys to keep them entertained.

Other Strange Behaviors

Slow Blinking

Another way that your kitten will communicate their love and acceptance of you is through blinking. When your soft bundle of fur sits quietly in front of you and stares at you with those big yellow eyes and either squints at you through half-closed eyes or slowly opens and closes their eyelids, you know you are in their good books. This is the cat equivalent of human kisses. You can usually "feel" their approval of you at those times, as it is quite a special, intimate moment between you and your beloved feline.

Seat Stealing

You will often find that when you get up out of your seat for a couple of minutes to go to the bathroom or put the kettle on, your cat is sitting in your chair when you return. When a cat steals your seat, it is just another way they are acknowledging that they feel connected to you and part of the same family unit. When you get up, you vacate a spot that is both warm and full of your scent. Since they love you, and they love warmth, they move straight into that spot. And they are always reluctant to give it up when you return.

Keyboard Walking

Another common cat behavior that can sometimes be annoying is a cat's propensity to walk across your computer keyboard as you are trying to type.

Whether you at your desk trying to get that report finished or sitting on the sofa doing some online shopping with your laptop, it seems that your cat knows how to interrupt you in the most inconvenient way. One minute you are typing away with proficiency, and the next minute your cat is literally sitting on your hands.

Why is that? Can they not see that we are busy and don't want to be interrupted? Do they not know that we don't want a whole string of percentage signs typed across the screen?

Well, of course, they have absolutely no idea about what we are doing with the computer; they just know that our hands are there, and our hands are moving. And if our hands are moving, they want to get in on the action and have those hands moving on them to stroke and caress them. It is quite smart on their part!

Bringing Gifts

As part of their natural hunting behavior, cats like to "catch" things and bring them to you, proud of their "kill." My cat likes to bring me tissues. She pulls a tissue from a Kleenex box somewhere around the house, chews it up a bit, and carries it in her mouth to the kitchen. She drops it on the kitchen floor and emits a particular "Meow" that she only uses for that purpose. That Meow says: "Here, I have caught something, and I have brought it to the kitchen for you because I know that is where you prepare the food."

Your cat might find some other type of object to bring you, but it will always find some way to contribute. If your cat is allowed outside and it happens to catch a bird or a mouse, it will bring it into where you prepare the food. It is just their way of trying to share the burden of supplying the food.

Boxes

Most cats love crawling under things and getting into tight spaces, but some cats seem to make it an art form. To that effect, you may find that your cat loves getting into cardboard boxes.

Some cats just love boxes: big boxes, small boxes, short boxes, long boxes – most cats are box-crazy! No sooner have you unpacked your latest online-shopping purchase that just arrived in the mail, when you look down and notice that your cat has already climbed in to the empty box! You often find them head-deep, with their backside sticking out as they try to squeeze into even the tiniest of boxes that they will never fit into!

As you get to know your cat you will discover other interesting things about them. In many ways, they are very much like humans: each cat has their own unique personality and quirks. Some are playful, some are gentle. Some are fussy, some are bossy. Some are stoic and serene, others are whimsical. Whatever personality your cat has, one thing is for sure – they will always love their owner!

Helping Your Birman Cat Deal with Shyness or Fear

Along with medical conditions, cats can end up with behavioral issues as a result of stress, anxiety and depression. They may also display OCD type behaviors caused by these problems.

It is important to know your cat's normal routines and behaviors so you can quickly spot problems when they first occur. If you know what to look for, you can help your cat either by soothing them or by having them treated by their veterinarian. "Bad" behavior often has a medical cause, such as an illness and the quicker the problem is found, the more likely it is for it to be treated successfully.

Even though the Birman cat adapts well to most situations they are in, not every cat has the same personality.

It isn't uncommon for some cats to be a little shy or standoffish, especially when thrust into a new environment.

If it is possible to do so, put your new family member into an area that you can close off with a baby gate so they can still see out into the rest of their new home. It will help them acclimate better to their new surroundings. In addition, you need to also interact with him or her as it will also help make their transition a smoother one.

Sometimes fear is mistaken for shyness because they can have the same root causes and the behaviors are almost the same. Fortunately, by being patient, you can help your new furry family member overcome their fear. Let the cat set his or her own pace because otherwise they may feel cornered and resort to fighting with you or other animals in the household.

Shyness or fear are not personality traits they have to be stuck with for the rest of their lives, especially if a medical condition is the underlying cause of their behavior.

Whenever you introduce a new cat into your home, regardless if you adopted it from a shelter or a breeder, you should make an appointment with the veterinarian you have chosen for your cat's care and have them examined. This allows any underlying medical issues to be discovered and quickly treated.

Even though you may have papers showing that your Wedgie has a clean bill of health, a check-up should still be performed. It is also a good way to introduce the vet to your cat.

Poor socialization is often another reason that a cat will display signs of fear or shyness. A kitten should be socialized with other cats, animals and humans starting at about six weeks old. However, if they were removed from their mother's care at a young age, they may not have been fully socialized.

A kitten should stay with its mother for at least eight weeks, although 12 weeks is better and they are usually fully socialized by that age.

Changes in the cat's environment can cause them to be scared or shy as well. Humans even get shy when they are introduced to a new environment, such as a new school or starting a new job, so it understandable that a cat moving into a new home may experience bouts of shyness or fear.

Don't be surprised if your new addition hides away for a few days until they are adjusted to their new environment. Some cats have been known to stay hidden up to two weeks.

Patience is the key in helping your new cat deal with its shyness. Gently pet him or her while speaking in a soothing voice to try to reassure the cat. Let them explore their new surroundings on their own, without forcing the issue. Birman cats easily adapt to new environments and if he or she is allowed to explore their new home on their terms, they will quickly get used to it.

Be sure they always have access to fresh water and a clean litter box. Put them on a feeding schedule and leave toys out so they can entertain themselves. As they get comfortable, they will begin to venture out further to explore their new surroundings and make themselves at home.

Some of the same causes of shyness will also trigger fear in some cats and a scared cat can sometimes react aggressively to humans and/or other animals. When you are trying to deal with a cat that is showing signs of fear, don't stare at him or her directly in the eyes. This is a sign of aggression for cats and it will trigger a "flight" or "fight" response. Most of the time, the cat will try to flee, unless it feels trapped and then it will start hissing, biting and clawing at you.

If you have other pets in your home, you need to introduce your new cat to your other pets gradually. Using a baby gate to block their access to the others will come in handy, especially if the cat is too small to leap or climb over the gate. The gate will allow them to see the other pets and get acquainted with them while keeping everyone safe.

Loud noises and environmental disasters may also trigger fear in cats. While the loud noises can be easily dealt with, an unexpected disaster can be problematic.

You will usually be aware of loud noises in your neighborhood and when they are scheduled to occur, such as construction, Fourth of July or New Year's Eve fireworks.

This will allow you to put your cat some place where they feel safe and where they can't hear any loud sounds.

If you live in an area that has tornadoes, hurricanes, fires or where other natural disasters may occur, be prepared with an evacuation kit for your Birman cat. The kit should include a cat carrier, enough food and water to last three to four days, a litter box, litter, something to calm them down when they are stressed and a favored toy or two. If you are prepared, it will be easier to deal with their fears and when you get back home, you can begin to soothe your cat's anxiety.

Fear and shyness are not the only psychological problems that can affect cats. They may also have problems with depression, OCD behaviors and stress. However, shyness and fear are two of the most common behaviors found in cats, even for breeds that normally have pleasant temperaments, such as the Birman cat. If you are patient with a shy or scared cat and show them love, they will normally overcome their shyness or fear.

Stop Your Cat From Scratching Furniture

You can keep your furniture intact, even if you have a cat! However, felines are notorious scratchers, thanks to the wildness embedded in their genes that makes them feel the need to scratch as they sharpen their nails for gripping prey.

They are notorious scratchers, sometimes for fun and to spite you, and sometimes to hone their gripping skill.

Whatever their reason for doing that is, you really don't want any scratches on your furniture. You can train your cat no to scratch.

For starters, you need to understand that all cats scratch objects because it is an instinctive and natural behavior. Even cats with trimmed claws tend to scratch as a way of communicating or as a displacement behavior.

Having a cat around means you have to be braced for some scratches on your expensive furniture here and there. What if you want to have your cake and eat it? Is it possible to keep a cat and your treasured furniture? The good news is that yes, you can have the best of both worlds but in order to do this, you might have to bring your beloved feline friend up to speed. If you wish to keep your antiques and give your cats a home, try these few steps;

1. Stop your cats right in their track every time you bust them scratching or attempting to scratch your furniture.

    Yelling at them will stop them at that particular moment, but it is not a permanent solution, as your cats will always scratch the furniture in your absence. Try an alternative. You can get wood or obsolete furniture that your cats can scratch all they want.

2. Shower your cats with affection and reward them for good behavior. Cats, just like kids, respond positively to affection and rewards. Rewarding

good behavior is also a guarantee that your feline friends will not scratch your furniture in your absence.

3.   Ensure that the targeted furniture is out of bounds for the cats. You can create a restricted area where the cats should not step in unless under supervision. These areas include the living room and the bedroom.

Lock those rooms when you are not in them. The cat should remain in its room when no one is in these restricted areas rooms in the house.

4.   Cats can be predictable at times. If you notice that your cat picks on certain furniture when on a scratching spree, you might need to shield the furniture with a double-sided tape. Alternatively, you could cover the target furniture with fabrics or sheets that are not claw-friendly.

This will discourage your cats from trying a clawing spree on such furniture. Don't try perching furniture on higher places because cats can jump.

5.   A horizontal scratcher on your rags can also come in handy. This will play a huge role in distracting the cats from scratching your treasured furniture. Ensure that the scratchers are made of material that your feline friend will enjoy scratching but avoid getting scratchers that have the same aesthetics as your rags or sofas.

When you find your cat scratching furniture, stop her in her tracks, immediately. Show your displeasure by talking to the cat in a low but very serious tone. Cats can read tone differences and are bound to know when you are angry. Don't let the cat get away with anything.

Preventing Aggressive Behavior

Aggressive behavior by your cat can be very frustrating. Aggression is one of the most common feline behavior problems, with inappropriate urination and biting topping the list. So, what to do when your cat acts aggressive? While some owners find their cat's aggressive behavior as normal and turn a blind eye to it, others find it inappropriate and look for ways to discipline them.

Well, problem behaviors can be successfully resolved through a combination of behavior triggers. Let's talk about some of the aggressive behaviors and triggers.

Cats have a natural instinct to stalk anything that moves. They love to strike and pounce on small objects that appear like a prey to them. This behavior is common in kittens, but you may find many adult cats also play hunt. If your kitten exhibits such behavior, it is better to discipline it once in a while; or else, it may eventually get out of control.

You can easily recognize exaggerated postures made by cats. It will help to identify these tantrums, which may include flattening their ears, crouching, dilated pupils, and tail swishing back and forth. It's important that you do not encourage rough play right from the beginning, which includes biting and scratching. However, it does not mean that you should use startling techniques to redirect the kitty's attention, as there is a fear that your techniques may make them feel shy and scared to interact with you.

Concentrate on making your interactions with your kitty fun and entertaining. Cats are known to become overly active if left alone, often becoming destructive when bored.

Understanding Cat Body Language

As a cat owner, it's important that you understand what your pet is trying to communicate through its body language. If you can accurately "read" your cats and understand their feelings why they do what they do, it will help you respond more effectively to their behavioral issues, of which aggression tops the list.

Though cat's body language can be hard to interpret, it might help to know what the cat's basic postures mean, helping you deal with behavior problems more effectively. Additionally, understanding their body language and motivations behind their actions will help you fully enjoy their company.

While a defensively aggressive cat appears self-protective and makes itself look smaller, an offensively aggressive cat tries to make itself look more intimidating and bigger. Whether a kitty is in a defensive or offensive posture, don't try to touch or punish them on such occasions.

It's important that you set up your kitty to succeed in learning good behavior so it can be rewarded. Remember, rewarding your kitty for exhibiting good behavior is one of the most effective ways of training a cat.

Set Up the Ideal Home Environment

Of course, you don't want your kitty to be a spoiled brat. So it is important that you create just the right environment in your home, ensuring the pet's misbehavior isn't a rewarding experience for them. Try to find something that your kitty isn't too fond of or does not like. This way you can use its dislike for certain things to your benefit and indirectly tell the kitty to stay away from your precious things, such as furniture.

Cats learn best in a positive environment, where there is a lot of praise and rewards, along with positive reinforcement.

Redirected Aggression

When a cat sees or hear something it can't access, it may become aroused and reactive enough to unleash a severe attack. Your cat might react to seeing another cat in the yard. If it can't reach the other cat, it would instantly lash out at a nearby human or even a pet. This kind of aggression is often misdiagnosed, as the actual source or trigger of the agitation is usually unknown. Cat owners call this type of aggression unprovoked, since they are left unaware about the trigger of their kitty's misbehavior.

Some of the common triggers include:

- Smelling odor of another cat somewhere – may be on a human or object
- Watching another cat passing by through a window
- Returning indoors after getting outside if it typically lives indoors
- Being frightened by a dog
- Hearing high-pitched noises

Petting-Induced Aggression

When a cat is showing such type of aggression, it does give a number of warning signs, which are often ignored by pet owners until it is too late. The situation may arise at times when you are petting your cat and it is beyond the cat's tolerance of petting. In such situations, the cat may react – lash out, scratch or bite you.

While petting may cause an over-stimulation, some of your stroking moves may feel uncomfortable to the kitty and it may react aggressively in the form of tail thumping, shifting body position, tail lashing, cessation of purring, or ear twitching.

It's important to learn about your cat's body language so you can remain cautious while petting and not cause it any kind of over-stimulation or frustration in order to avoid petting-induced aggression.

Inter-cat Aggression

If you bring a new kitten to your home when you already own one, you can create a situation for inter-cat aggression. The two may start seeing each other as a hostile entity and may start challenging each other for territory, while the old cat sees it as an invasion into its existing territory, the new one starts to try and claim its dominance.

Fear Aggression

As its name suggests, this type of aggression is rooted in fear. If your cat is displaying fear aggression, it is best to leave it alone, without interacting. Provide it with a place where it can feel secure and comfortable. It may help to find out what is triggering its fear.

Play-Related Aggression

This type of aggression affects cats that have been separated from their littermates too early. An orphaned cat may also exhibit this type of aggression, as it has been denied social play and kept separate from its family.

The best way to correct such type of aggression is to use interactive toys for play sessions. Do not use your hands as toys. Teach your kitten that biting your hands will bring an end to the playtime session.

Aggression toward Humans

Some cats may grow up fearful and aggressive toward humans if they were not properly handled, socialized, and trained in the beginning of their life. Such cats are wary of humans, easily get upset and threaten their owners.

Frightened cats assume a crouched position, with tails curled inward. In such situations, you will see their ears in a back position and their bodies tilted away from what they perceive as threat. It is common for them to lash out or bite whatever approaches them.

Ideally, cats show such kind of behavior when they are brought to new surroundings. Some kittens do show such behavior when approached by a stranger. Some cats may hiss and their eyes may become dilated.

Do not let their negative behavior be ingrained in your feline's personality. Make sure you get your cat socialized when they are still young. It helps to get them used to being touched.

The best time to train your kitty is when it is relaxed and content. It may help to begin by scratching and rubbing its head, without making any sudden moves, and gradually stroking its back and tail. You may want to indulge in sweet talk while doing this. It's important to look for any signs of the cat feeling frustrated or agitated. Reward the kitty with a food treat at the end of the session if it stays calm throughout the training period.

Walking Your Birman Cat

It isn't the most common thing to notice a cat being walked with a leash. Typically, it is dogs that have leashes and cats that wander free. Nevertheless, nowadays, with many little animals and birds on the brink of extinction, you might wish to think about teaching your cat or kitty to walk on a leash. This is going to stop the cat from hunting down and eliminating little birds or butterflies. It is going to stop it from climbing trees to take baby birds from their nests. It is going to additionally keep it out of harm, as you are going to be monitoring its location in a responsible way.

Instead of simply utilizing a leash and a collar to walk your cat, consider utilizing a harness. A cat's head is rather little in comparison to the remainder of it, and a collar might be inclined to pull over its head and off. The harness straps ought to surround the body and the neck simply behind the front legs, with 2 more straps to join the circles together, one down the rear of the neck and one through the front legs. You are going to need a clip for the leash too. Light leather or artificial material is excellent for a cat's harness. Do not utilize anything too bulky, or the cat is going to decline it.

It's additionally essential to get your cat accustomed to the feel and look of the leash prior to you taking it for a walk in it. After the cat has actually ended up being used to seeing the leash (you might leave it in its bed), then let it don it for a couple of minutes every day prior to leading it around by the lead. While still inside, yank lightly on the lead whilst calling your cat. When it comes to you, commend the cat, however never ever scold or force it if it does not come, or it'll believe the leash is a penalty.

As you walk your cat with a leash, do not walk the cat as you would a doggy. Doggies like to run quickly and are more than delighted to trot at a good gait next to you when they have learned to lead. Cats are rather distinct. They do not normally walk or run quickly in a straight line. They have a tendency to stop and go, to wander, and to check unusual rustlings in the grass. For your cat to take pleasure in walking outside with you, you need to permit it to do at least a few of these things. Never ever yank the cat along harshly. The cat is going to be very likely to back off extremely rapidly. Carefully urge it to come with you and applaud it when it moves in the appropriate direction. Hold out snacks for the cat as you call it to come.

Cats additionally feel the heat quickly. Don't expect to opt for a fast run around the block. Keep in mind that the cat has no shoes for protection from the scorching heat or cold snow. Walk your cat on the grass and in the shade whenever possible. Sun is okay if it's not really that hot.

Regard your cat's requirement to rest as you are walking it. It's a good idea to halt and smell the roses yourself. Let your walk remain in a calm and worry-free environment. Your cat is going to likely be scared of skateboarders zooming past or a loud traffic. With these handful of tips, your cat ought to quickly start to enjoy his everyday walk.

Training Your Birman Cat to Survive Outdoors

Staying outdoors requires a set of survival skills for any animal, including cats. Although cats have been domesticated for many generations, their ancestors used to be in the wild. As a result, they inherit instincts that help them survive outdoors. This natural heritage will help your domesticated cat to survive outdoors with some helpful training.

Some cats find living outdoors much easier than living indoors. The fact that cats are independent creatures makes living outdoors easier for them. However, outdoor cats require training to ensure their safety and well-being. They should be trained to come inside when the weather is bad. Some cat owners prefer to have their cats come in every night.

Cats can run into many dangers when they are outside. Therefore, it does not matter if a cat spends most of her day outdoors or if it's only limited to a few hours every day, her owner needs to make sure that she is healthy and safe.

Tip One: Inform the Neighbors

It's a good idea to let the neighbors know when a cat is being trained to stay in the yard. Make sure that they understand that the cat will be trained to stay in her yard but to gently chase her away in case she wanders onto their property.

Tip Two: Check the Cat's Vaccination Record

Outdoor cats can run wild animals who might have rabies. Therefore, a cat needs to have up-to-date vaccinations before she is trained to stay outdoors. Some local laws may dictate additional vaccines that need to be given to outdoor cats. Therefore, it's advised that owners check such local laws before letting their cat spend time in the yard unsupervised.

Tip Three: Secure the Yard

Cat fence barriers are the best when it comes to securing a yard so that a cat can be provided with a safe yard from which she cannot escape. However, cat fence barriers require pre-existing walls and fencing. They can also be placed around areas that the cat shouldn't wander into such as large trees, gates, and sheds.

Cat enclosures, on the other hand, provide limited outdoor space for cats. They do not require pre-existing boundaries such as fences and walls. Some cat enclosures feature cat runs, tunnels, and pens. They provide a lot of flexibility for cat owners who want to provide their cats with some outdoor time every day.

Another option is to construct a cat patio. They transform existing outdoor lounges and patios into secure outdoor areas for cats. Cat patios made using steel offer ultimate security to ensure that cats are safe during the time they spend outdoors.

Tip Four: Prepare for Cat Fights

Other cats who belong to neighbors or stray cats may come face-to-face with your cat when she spends time outdoors. As a result, owners need to be prepared to break up catfights. A good way to break up a catfight is to use a spray bottle or a water gun. Keep these tools handy when the cat is outdoors just in case. However, this method should only be used as a last resort. It should not be used to discourage behaviors other than catfights.

Tip Five: Establish a Method to Invite the Cat In and Out of the House

It's important to come up with a sound method to bring the cat in and out of the house. The best way to achieve this goal is to train her to come when called. However, some cat owners use rewards and toys to lure cats in and out of their homes.

Tip Six: Keep Outdoor Sessions Short

A cat shouldn't be kept out in the yard for long periods when she is starting training. Keep the sessions short and consistent. She should be supervised at all times when she is in the yard during training. Her outdoor time can be gradually increased as she becomes more comfortable outside while respecting the boundaries.

Tip Seven: Avoid Taking the Cat Out Right After Waking Up

It's advised that owners do not take their cats out as soon as they wake up. Doing so encourages cats to wake up their owners very early in the morning. Therefore, spend at least an hour after they wake up before allowing the cat to go out into the yard. Also, it's advised that cats aren't taken out at night or during twilight hours.

Training a Birman Cat to Stay in the Yard

Most cat owners tend to keep their cats indoors. However, training them to spend some time outside can be beneficial for both owners and cats alike as long as the yard is secure. It helps cats to spend their pent-up energy exploring the yard and avoid the development of behavioral issues that can be frustrating, inconvenient, and even harmful to owners.

Training a Birman cat to spend time outdoors becomes much easier if they are taught to come when they are called. They should also understand how the clicker works. It's recommended that a cat is trained to walk with a harness on before training them to spend time in the yard.

Step One: Make the Cat Familiar with the Yard

It's important to first introduce the Birman cat to the yard. It needs to be done gradually while ensuring that the cat is relaxed and doesn't run away. It is advised that the owner picks a time where the cat is quiet and calm to follow this step in the cat's training. Choosing a time that the cat usually sleeps is a good way to ensure that they won't have much pent-up energy that makes training difficult.

Get the cat to come near the door by calling her name. Gently put the harness on and secure it to the leash. Reward her for remaining calm. Gently pick her up and step outside. Give her a reward for being calm. If the cat remains calm, place her on the ground with her facing the house.

Picking up the Birman cat lets her know that the owner is in control and placing her on the ground with her facing the house reduces the chances of her running away. Allow the cat a few seconds to feel the ground and sniff around. Offer her a reward for being calm on the ground. Then pick her up and walk into the house.

Step Two: Gradually Increase the Time That the Cat is Left on the Ground

Slowly increase how long the Birman cat is placed on the ground. She should be wearing the harness during training to ensure that she doesn't run away. Picking her up and placing her down during training helps by getting her used to being handled when being outdoors. As the amount of time increases, make sure to pet her in between. It reminds her that the owner is around and in charge. Pick her up, hold her for around 10 seconds, and put her down in between. Repeat this step near the house until the cat calmly stays on the ground for a few minutes without trying to run away.

Step Three: Gradually Increase the Distance From the House

Now that the Birman cat can spend at least five minutes without trying to run away from the owner, it's time to increase the distance that she's allowed to go from the house. Start taking a few steps further every day until reaching the farthest boundary of the yard. It's important not to rush through this step. The cat should always know that the owner is in charge and the end destination should be the house. If she tries to escape, gently stop her using the leash, pick her up, and bring her inside. Do not try to do any more training that day.

Step Four: Get the Cat to Follow the Owner Towards the House

Now that the Birman cat has learned to stay calm when put down on the ground while being outdoors, it's time to train her to follow the owner to the house. When it's time to go inside, take a few steps toward the house and see if the cat follows. If she does, sound the clicker and reward her with a treat. If she doesn't, place a treat on the ground. When she comes and takes the treat, sound the clicker, and reward her.

Repeat this until the cat starts to follow the owner all the way into the house. Gradually increase the number of steps taken towards the house before a reward is offered. Give her a treat and praise her as soon as she comes inside too. Repeat this step until the cat follows the owner inside without needing any encouragement with rewards.

Step Five: Get the Cat to Follow the Owner Outside

Train the Birman cat to follow the owner outside using the same approach in step four. Make sure to call out her name when stepping outside. Reward her appropriately for desirable behavior. By the end of this step, the cat should reach a stage where she follows the owner outside without trying to run away.

Step Six: Offer More Freedom

Go into the yard with the Birman cat and place the leash on the ground. See how she responds. Reward her for not wandering too far away or stepping towards the owner. End training if she goes towards the boundaries of the yard. Avoid letting her go too far. The owner should only be far enough so that he/she can grab the leash if the cat tries to escape. Repeat this step until the cat doesn't run away too far when the leash is placed down. She should always understand that the owner is still in control.

Step Seven: Remove the Leash

When an owner is certain that the cat will not try to run away and that she knows to stay away from the boundaries of the yard, the leash can be slowly removed. Remove the leash, let a few seconds pass, put it back on, and reward the cat. Repeat this step while increasing the amount of time that the cat stays without the leash. Reward her for being calm.

Then, remove the leash and take a step back. Give her a few seconds and call her. When she returns to the owner, sound the clicker, and offer a treat. Repeat this step until the owner is sure that the cat will obey his command to come to him/her when she is called. If she is responding well, the owner can gradually increase the distance from the cat.

Step Eight: Monitor Until the Cat Is Fully Trained

Gradually give more freedom to the Birman cat until she reaches a point where she can be let out with the owner staying by the door. The cat should return to the owner and follow him/her inside when called. Never leave the cat in the yard unattended until she is fully trained.

Training a Cat to Ring a Bell to Come Inside |

Letting a Birman cat stay in the yard is great as long as it is made secure so that the cat can't escape. Proper training can also make sure that the cat stays away from boundaries such as walls and fences without attempting to escape. When a cat is trained to stay in the yard, owners can let her stay there and attend to their work indoors. However, the cat may want to come in while the owners are busy. Therefore, establishing a way to alert the owners is a great way to make sure that the cat can come inside when they have had enough outdoor time.

Training a Birman cat to ring a bell is a great way to help her alert the owners to let her inside. It makes sure that the cat isn't forced to spend time outdoors when she doesn't want to (which might discourage her from going outside later). It also gives owners the peace of mind to go about their household duties knowing that they will know if their cats want to come in. '

Step One: Introduce the Bell to the Cat

Purchase a bell that is loud enough to alert anyone inside. Attach a string to it and hang it inside the door until the training lasts. It can later be moved outside. The cat should be able to easily touch the bell whenever she wants to.

Bring the cat near to the door and bring the bell close to their face. When she sniffs or touches the bell to inspect it, sound the clicker, and offer her a treat. Repeat this step until the cat starts sniffing or touching the bell and looks at the owner in anticipation of a treat. When she does that, it's a great sign that she has started to associate interacting with the bell as something rewarding.

Step Two: Get the Cat to Touch the Bell

Now that the Birman cat knows that sniffing or touching the bell wins her a treat, it's time to encourage her only to touch it instead of sniffing it. Start pointing at the bell to get her to interact with it. When she sniffs or touches it, sound the clicker, and give her a treat. Gradually decrease the times she is rewarded for sniffing the bell. Eventually, the cat should only be rewarded for touching the bell.

Step Three: Get the Cat to Ring the Bell

The bell should ring most of the instances the Birman cat touches it. Gradually limit the rewards to only when the bell rings. Limit rewarding the cat for touching the bell without making it ring. This step makes it clear to the cat that she is supposed to ring the bell instead of simply touching it. By the end of this step, the cat should only expect a treat when she rings the bell.

Step Four: Associate the Opening of the Door With the Ringing of the Bell

This step helps the Birman cat understand that the door opens every time she rings the bell. Get the cat to ring the bell, open the door, and reward her. She will soon understand that ringing the bell makes the door open. Repeat this step until the cat starts looking at the door after ringing the bell.

Step Five: Hang the Bell Outside

Now it's time to hang the bell outside. Hang it near the door, then take the Birman cat outside and point at the bell. Open the door as soon as she rings it, open the door, and place a treat inside the house. Then close the door. Repeat this step until the cat understands the sequence of these events. She will soon understand that ringing the bell opens the door and that she is supposed to come in when it does.

Training a Birman Cat to Use a Cat Door

A cat door is a great way to allow your cat the freedom to leave and enter the home as they please, without requiring someone in the home to open and close doors to let them in and out. However, a cat door can only be allowed once a yard has been made completely secure and the cat has been trained to stay in the yard.

Cat doors can be more freely used if more secure cat outdoor fencing such as cat patios and enclosures are used, instead of letting cats roam freely in yards. Most cats figure out how to use cat doors by themselves. However, some cats may require some help from their owners in the form of training. Let's look at a few steps that will help your cat be a more successful cat door user.

Step One: Get the Cat to Go In and Out of the Fully Open Cat Door

Hold the Birman cat door fully open. Place a treat just outside the cat door so that the cat only needs to pop her head out of the door to grab it. Sound the clicker as soon as the kitty pushes her head out of the cat door and then quickly offer her another reward. Repeat this step until the cat is fully comfortable peeking through the cat door.

Step Two: Get the Cat to Leave and Return Through the Fully Open Cat Door

Start increasing the distance between the door and the treat. Eventually, the treat should be placed far enough that the cat needs to move her entire body out of the cat door. Sound the clicker as soon as she moves all the way through the door to get the treat. Place another treat inside the house at the same distance. Sound the clicker and offer another treat when the cat returns through the cat door to get it.

Step Three: Gradually Start Closing the Cat Door

Gradually close the door while repeating Step Two. Eventually, the Birman cat will need to push her way through the cat door to get to her treat. The closing of the door should happen bit by bit so that the cat doesn't notice it. Eventually, she will get used to pushing her way through the fully closed cat door to get to the rewards that await on the other side.

Training a Cat to Hunt

Have a pesky mouse that you're looking to your cat for some help with? Giving your kitty a little nudge through some training will help.

Most domestic cats are great hunters, thanks to natural instincts passed on by their ancestors. Before domestication, cats were born in the wild and had to hunt to survive. Even after generations and generations of domestication, cats still carry their hunting instincts. As a result, training a cat to hunt can be done quite easily.

Kittens learn the basics of hunting from their mothers. However, many domestic cats do not stay with their mothers long enough to learn these skills. Therefore, the owners need to help them gain hunting skills during kittenhood so that they grow up to become competent hunters. Even most adult cats can be trained to hunt since they have the natural inbred instinct to do so.

When it comes to training Birman cats to hunt mice, the owners need to find a few toys that look similar to mice. They can be used to train cats to hunt. Doing so makes it easier for cats to translate those experiences into hunting real mice later on.

Step One: Coaching Hunting and Stalking Instincts

Cats stalk their prey before pouncing on them at the most opportune moment. Therefore, it's an instinct that is crucial for them to become great hunters. Stalking and hunting instincts are better coached during kittenhood. However, adult cats can also be coached or rather "reminded" of their natural hunting and stalking instincts although it may take more work.

The best way to sharpen a cat's hunting and stalking skills is to use toys that can mimic the movement of small prey. Small balls and string toys can be pulled around by the owner. Most kittens and cats quickly respond by stalking and pouncing on them using similar actions that would be incorporated while hunting. You can help to heighten your kitty's reflexes by using toys to sharpen a cat's natural hunting instincts during playtime every day.

Step Two: Present Them with Dead Carcasses of Ideal Prey

Okay - now this one does get a little gross. But it's a big help with getting your Birman cat to understand the goal. One of the best ways to help a cat understand the process of hunting prey is to present her with a carcass of the type of creature that the owner wishes the cat to hunt. For example, presenting a cat with the carcass of a mouse can make it clear to her that she should hunt mice. Mother cats use the same approach to train their kittens to hunt. So, the next time you catch a mouse in a trap, gently release it on the floor in front of your kitty to let her smell it and bat it around a bit before you throw it away. It won't take long for her instincts to kick in and for her to understand.

Step Three: Provide Encouragement When a Cat Presents "Gifts"

Cats often bring their kills to their owners as gifts. Sue, it's not exactly the kind of gift you want to open, but the kitty will still be very proud and seek your encouragement. So just be prepared for when such a gift is dropped at your feet and gush with some positive reinforcement to encourage them to continue hunting. Be sure to reward her with something she likes such as praise, petting, lap-time, or treats.

Chapter Seven: Vet Care for Your Birman Cat

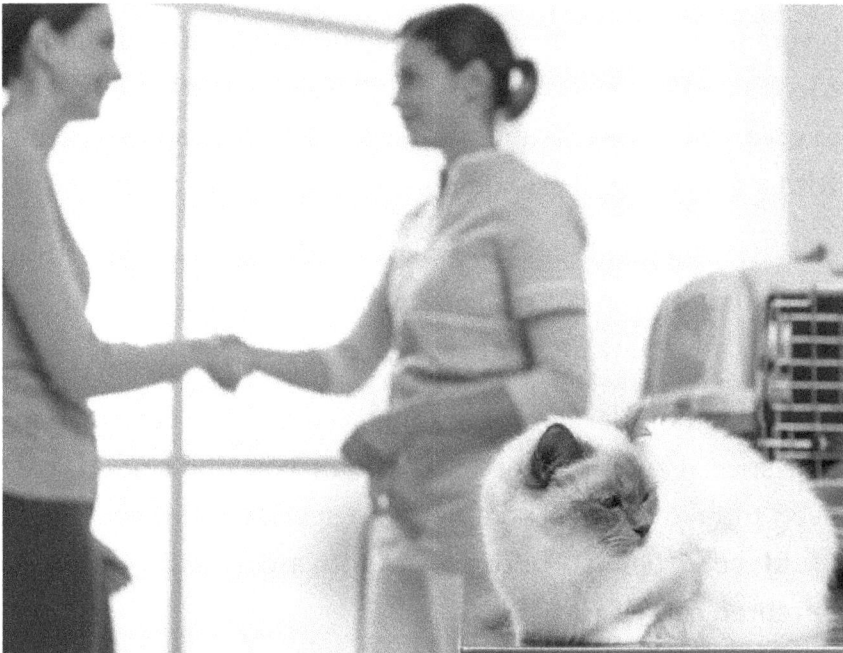

How to Find a Good Vet for Your Birman Cat

Your cat's veterinarian will be your partner in helping you keep your cat healthy and happy, so it is important to find a vet that you can trust to properly treat your cat. A vet not only needs to be good with animals, but they should also be people oriented in order to instruct and help pet owners properly care for their furry companions.

You shouldn't wait until you have a medical emergency to find a vet; you should choose your vet before you bring the new family addition home.

A good way to find a veterinarian is to ask the pet lovers in your life for vet recommendations. If your family, friends and coworkers have a vet they like, they will be glad to give you a referral and, if they have had a bad experience with a vet, you will also quickly hear about their experience.

It is a good way to either quickly eliminate vets from consideration for your Birman kitten or find those you will need to interview for your cat's care.

In most larger communities, there are veterinarians that specialize in cat care. Although you don't necessarily need to take your cat to a vet who specializes in cat care, it could be a better option since you are bringing home a purebred cat.

Cat veterinarians have been trained how to handle cats and educated about the various diseases that affect them. If you happen to live in an area with cat specialists available to you, consider interviewing them to handle for your cat's care.

The veterinarian is only one member of a team that will be responsible for your cat's medical care. Usually in the vet's office, there will be technicians, vet assistants, caretakers and other support staff that will also be responsible for part of your cat's care. When you go interview the veterinarian, you should also evaluate the support staff's ability to handle your cat in a caring, competent manner.

Although it shouldn't be your first or only consideration for selecting a vet, ask about their fee schedule for check-ups, treatment and emergency care so you can compare them with the other veterinarians you are considering.

Find out if they offer senior or multiple pet discounts, if applicable to your situation. Check to see how far of a drive the vet's office is from your home to determine how long it would take to get there in an emergency. Driving a few miles out of your way or paying a slightly higher free may be well worth the effort in order to find a great vet for your Birman cat.

Conduct an online search for cat hospitals and other veterinarians as well. Most businesses today have websites to promote their services and you can find contact information, hours of operation, information about their services and sometimes there is staff information too. The Internet is a great resource when you are looking for a veterinarian or general information about Birman cats.

When you have a list of veterinarians to interview to become your cat's doctor, check to see if they have accreditation with the American Animal Hospital Association. The accreditation process for the AAHA is voluntary and it shows that the vets who are accredited meet the association's standards for the quality care of animals and that their facility and equipment have met the AAHA's standards as well.

Should you ever need to take your cat to a specialist, find out if they have been board certified. Certification requires an additional two to four years of study, depending on their area of expertise, and they also have to pass a rigorous examination in order to finalize their certification.

If the specialist is not board certified, dismiss them from consideration for your pet's care, if you have a choice. Depending on the specialty, you may have to take your cat there any way if there isn't another specialist in your area.

Once you have your final list of veterinarians that you are considering, schedule an appointment to meet them and tour their facility. Meeting with the vet will let you evaluate their ability to discuss medical matters with you and help you start building a rapport with them.

During the tour, meet with members of the support staff and try to evaluate their ability to talk with pet owners and handle pets as well. Most vets will be happy to give you a tour of their offices and pet care areas and if they are reluctant, be wary because that could be a sign that they are hiding something from their clients.

Take a list of questions that you may have with you so you don't forget to ask them. Find out if the vet has had any experience treating a Birman cat and, if they have, that will be a big plus in their favor as these cats are not that common in the United States.

Be sure to ask questions about the facility's policies and find out the vet's philosophy about treating pets, euthanasia and other concerns that you have.

Making a visual inspection of the facility during the tour will give you a lot of good information. It will allow you to observe its cleanliness, how well organized it is kept and whether it looks comfortable for the pets being treated. If the facility has dog and cat patients, find out if the cages are kept separate or if they are kept in the same room.

If you see something you don't like about the facility, don't be afraid to ask questions about it.

Find out how much of their testing is done in-house and whether you would need to take your pet to a specialist to have an EKG, x-ray, ultrasound or other testing done on your cat.

Also, find out if they have lab facilities onsite to analyze blood work or if it is sent to an outside lab. If it is sent out to a lab, that could delay test results, which could be crucial if your cat is seriously ill. Find out if they are available for emergency care and which emergency services they offer.

After you've selected the veterinarian you intend on bringing your cat to for care, play your part in the team effort to keep your cat healthy. Schedule an appointment for your new kitten so the vet can start building a rapport with both you and your new family member. By taking your cat to the vet for regular check-ups, it allows the vet to get to know your cat so he or she can better treat it when your cat is sick.

Observing your cat will help you get to know their normal routine and behaviors. This will make it easier to detect when your cat isn't feeling well or has been injured. Don't wait until your cat gets worse to call the vet, call their office as soon as you notice something wrong with your cat. Having your cat tested right away can be essential in being able to successfully treat them. Time is of the essence when a cat is ill and it is important that treatment is started right away. Waiting could be fatal for them in many cases.

Whenever you do transport your cat to the vet, take him or her in a cat carrier. Many cats do not like to travel in a car, even for just a few blocks and using a cat carrier will help protect both them and you. Bring them home in a cat carrier so it can start getting used to being in the carrier when you need to use it. Some cats will quickly take to it and even be curious enough when you open it to voluntarily walk into it and investigate the carrier.

Between the time you pick out your kitten and get to take him or her home, you should have ample opportunity to research, interview and decide whom you will use as your cat's veterinarian. Along with taking your cat in for regular check-ups and shots, you should be a caring, responsible pet owner whenever you visit the vet's office.

Keep control of your cat, ask questions and get to know the staff taking car of your furry family member. Developing a good relationship with your vet and the staff will help in keeping your cat healthy throughout its life.

Vaccinations

What is a Vaccine?

A vaccine is basically a solution containing antigens that to the body's immune system looks like a disease-causing organism but is not. Your cat can be given a vaccine orally or through injection. When introduced into the body, the vaccine stimulates the body's complex immune system, making the system strong enough to fight any disease-causing organism that enters the body. Having your cat vaccinated is therefore very important.

Different jurisdictions have different vaccine requirements for all pets including cats. While some vaccines are only available in particular regions of the world because of prevalence of specific cat diseases, others are only available in other regions. There are basically two types of vaccines; core and non-core vaccines. While core vaccines are mandatory to all cats regardless of region or location, non-core vaccines are only found in specific regions or locations.

Like with anything introduced into the body, vaccines present several symptoms including fever, vomiting, loss of appetite, sluggishness, diarrhea and swelling around injection area. There are also serious symptoms that may occur depending on the kind of vaccine your cat receives. These include life-threatening allergic reactions and development of tumor around injected area. The serious symptoms are however limited in occurrence. Vaccine symptoms are generally mild and do fade away within a fed day.

Safety of Vaccines

Although cat vaccines are generally safe, there has been controversy around some vaccines that are often considered unnecessary. You need to appreciate the fact that it is because of feline vaccines that cats can now live beyond their expected life-span. Production and administration of most vaccines that had raised controversies have luckily ceased. It is therefore perfectly safe to take your Birman cat to a vet to receive the core vaccines. In any case, you are most likely to buy a Birman kitten that is already vaccinated.

One major challenge that many cat owners face is when to have their cats vaccinated. There are different circumstances and instances when your Birman cat needs to be vaccinated.

Kitten Vaccination

Your Birman kitten or cat is most likely to have received its first vaccination while still with the breeder you bought it from. Even so, the vaccination must have been several weeks after it was born. This is because kittens naturally acquire sufficient immunity from their mothers through milk. Furthermore, a kitten's immune system is still not yet fully developed to receive artificial vaccination. Breeders do arrange with veterinarians for their kittens to be vaccinated once they attain the age of seven weeks with additional vaccinations administered when they are twelve and again once they attain the age of sixteen years. The two additional vaccinations are in most cases boosters that fortify the first vaccination.

Adult Cat Immunization

Adult cats are not vaccinated but rather immunized. Like with vaccination, immunization is aimed at further boosting your cat's immune system to continue being effective in offering protection against possible infections.

Core Cat Vaccines

Core cat vaccines are those that all cats should receive regardless of location. These vaccines are very effective in offering protection against life-threatening diseases found in all regions of the world. They include:

Feline Viral Rhinotracheitis (FVR) Vaccine

FVR Vaccine is administered to protect against FVR virus that is at times referred to as feline influenza or feline pneumonia. This is a respiratory disease found across the globe.

FVR is a highly contagious disease that can kill kittens within a few days of infection. The disease is easily transmitted through direct contact. One cat passes the disease on to another cat through saliva, nasal and eye secretions. When infected, your cat will most likely show such signs as coughing, sneezing, excessive nasal discharge, loss of appetite and high fever.

Feline Calicivirus (FCV) Vaccine

Your cat receives this vaccination to protect itself against the virus that causes respiratory infection. Occurrence of this disease usually ends in epidemic in areas with large cat populations because of its highly contagious nature.

FCV presents such symptoms as nose/eye discharge, mouth ulceration, anorexia and general body weakness at the initial stage. If affected, your cat is most likely to present such secondary symptoms as jaundice, high fever, swelling of the face and limbs (oedema) and dysfunction of organs within the body.

Feline Panleukopenia Virus (FPV) Vaccine

FPV vaccine is one of the most important cat vaccines that your cat must receive. This is because the vaccine offers protection against the highly contagious and fatal diseases caused by Panleukopenia virus that causes low white blood cells. The disease is largely transmitted through contact with body fluids of an infected cat.

If infected, your cat is most likely to show signs of severe dehydration, bloody diarrhea, anemia, depression, vomiting, loss of appetite, self-biting and loss of skin elasticity among other signs. Pregnant cats affected by the disease do give birth to kittens with cerebellar hypoplasia.

Feline Immunodeficiency Virus (FIV) Vaccine

FIV is often referred to as feline AIDS. This is so because it is in many ways similar to human immunodeficiency virus (HIV). There are different types of FIV that the FIV Vaccine is designed to protect against. Like in humans, your cat is most likely to live with FIV in case of infection in which case it will now be a carrier of the virus.

FIV attacks the immune system just in the same way that HIV does in humans. Although FIV and HIV are similar, humans cannot contract FIV and cats cannot contract HIV. Should your cat be infected, it will henceforth transmit the virus to other cats through saliva. Outdoor cats happen to be more at risk of contracting FIV virus compared to indoor cats.

Non-Core Cat Vaccines

Although classified as non-core cat vaccines, vaccines in this category are core in some regions of the world. This is because they are designed to offer cats protection against specific diseases only found in such regions. They include:

Feline Leukaemia Virus (FLV) Vaccine

FLV is a virus that causes life-threatening diseases in cats. One common disease associated with the virus is leukaemia, which develops when the virus destroys blood cells, in effect making them cancerous. The virus presents several symptoms including loss of appetite, poor coat condition, skin infections, fatigue, oral infections including gingivitis, diarrhoea and jaundice among many other symptoms. Your cat, if infected, will be able to transmit the virus to other cats through saliva, litter box (sharing) and food/water dishes.

Rabies Vaccine

Rabies was in the past a universal medical condition that affected humans, dogs and other warm-blooded animals such as cats. Vaccination campaigns undertaken in specific regions of the world made it possible for the disease to be eradicated in such regions. Rabies vaccine is now only common in specific regions where cats, dogs and humans are still vulnerable to Rabies infection.

Rabies is a serious disease that you should protect your Birman cat from by ensuring that it receives the necessary vaccination. It is a viral disease that causes serious inflammation of the brain. It presents such symptoms as fever, loss of consciousness and restricted movement among other symptoms. Most rabies cases do result in death.

Chlamydophila Felis Vaccine

Chlamydophila Felis is a bacteria commonly found in cats. The vaccine for the bacteria is designed to protect against it. The bacteria cause inflammation of a cat's conjunctiva, rhinitis and respiratory health problems.

Depending on your location, you may be required from time to time to take your cat to a local vet for specific vaccinations aimed at preventing identified cat diseases in your specific area. Such vaccinations are in most cases occasioned by outbreak of cat diseases. Different countries have legislated legislations that make such vaccinations mandatory and failure to adhere to the same attracts different penalties.

Apart from being a requirement of legislation, you need to consider your cat's vaccination seriously. This is because you are the ultimate beneficiary knowing that your cat is fully vaccinated or immunized and therefore well protected from diseases that can affect its health. It is therefore very important that you consult your local vet on a regular basis for proper information on cat vaccinations and immunizations.

Common Birman Cat Illnesses

If your Birman cat behaving oddly or showing signs of discomfort or ill health, it is important to find out what may be causing it. The sooner you discover your Birman cat's illness, the quicker it can be treated and the less discomfort and pain your cat will be put in. Cats are hardy animals and try to hide their symptoms of ill health for as long as they possibly can, making it more difficult to spot any changes. This section will guide you through the most common illnesses in Birman cats and the symptoms and treatments for each.

Arthritis and Joint Pain

What is it?

Arthritis is an abnormal change in your cat's joints. These changes occur when the cartilage around the joint, is worn away quicker than it can be replaced. Cartilage is used to protect the bone and prevents discomfort when moving. When Cartilage wears away, the joints can become painful and swollen and causes the bones to rub together, causing inflammation. Arthritis is most common in middle aged and senior cats, but can occur in younger cats. If untreated arthritis can be very painful for your cat and will reduce its quality of life. Although arthritis is incurable, early treatment can help reduce further cartilage loss, so it is important to seek a veterinarian's advice as soon as you spot any signs of arthritis. Certain cat breeds are more prone to arthritis than others; these tend to be the Siamese, Persian and Himalayan. Overweight cats are also more likely to get arthritis than a healthy weight cat, due to the extra strain the joints and put under.

Symptoms

A cat with arthritis may show some or all of these signs:

- Trouble jumping up or down onto surfaces
- Decreased activity
- Defecating outside the litter box
- Walking more stiffly than usual
- Limping
- Being less social

Treatment

Cats with arthritis should be put on a healthy, balanced diet and exercise should be encouraged as much as possible. They should also be put on a pain relief/anti-inflammatory medication; your veterinarian will advise as to which. There are a number of therapies that are also available to reduce arthritic pain. These are acupuncture, massage and hydrotherapy.

Allergic Dermatitis

What is it?

Allergic Dermatitis is a reaction to the skin caused by an allergy. Like humans, cats can also have allergies. Allergic Dermatitis is caused by allergies which will affect the skin. Allergies can be caused by the food your cat eats or something within the environment they live in. Cats can also be allergic to the bites of fleas and other parasites. Cats of any age to develop Allergic Dermatitis and it could be caused by a change to your cat's diet or environment. It is important to seek a veterinarian's advice if you spot any symptoms.

Symptoms

A cat with Allergic Dermatitis may show some or all of these signs:

- Itchy skin, particularly around the face and feet
- A foul odor emanating from the skin
- Red bumps on the skin
- Darkened skin, which may feel thicker than usual
- Thinning of the fur or fur loss
- Frequent shaking of the head

Treatment

The first course of action when your cat is confirmed to have allergic dermatitis is to find what is causing it. Depending on what is causing it, depends on what action will be taken. In a general environment allergy case, you will be advised to remove what is causing the allergic reaction from the environment and a topical cream can be given to relieve your cat's itchy and painful skin. Your cat will also be given antihistamines to manage the allergy.

Cat Flu

What is it?

Cat flu is a viral infection of the upper respiratory tract. Adult cats which were previously healthy are usually able to overcome the illness, but it can cause death in kittens and older cats with weaker immune systems.

Symptoms

A cat with cat flu may show some or all of these signs:

Sneezing

- Discharge from the nose (early stage it will be clear and then change to a green color)
- Conjunctivitis
- Rhinitis (Inflamed nasal lining)
- Fever
- Depression
- Can become dehydrated

- Loss of appetite

Treatment

Your cat will need to be kept as comfortable as possible and will require extensive nursing and monitoring. Each symptom of cat flu will be treated differently. Dehydrated cats may need to be put on a drip, discharge from the eyes and nose must be bathed frequently with warm salty water, conjunctivitis will be treated with the appropriate medication, depression will lessen as your cats health improves and a cats appetite will usually return with health.

Conjunctivitis

What is it?

Conjunctivitis is the inflammation of the moist tissue in a cat's eye. Other viruses can cause conjunctivitis to develop, the most common being the herpes virus and cat flu. Cats that are exposed to other cats with conjunctivitis are also more prone to develop the disease. Allergies can also cause conjunctivitis or it could be as simple as a particle lodged within the eye. Purebred cats are more expected to develop the disease than other cats.

Symptoms

A cat with conjunctivitis may show some or all of these signs:

- Discharge from the eyes

- Red, watery or crusty eyes
- Persistent squinting

Treatment

Conjunctivitis is usually treated with a medication and is most commonly treated on an outpatient basis. If it was caused by a foreign particle in the eye, then surgery may be needed to remove the lodging.

Cystitis

What is it?

Cystitis is the inflammation or infection of the bladder. It can be caused by a bacterial infection, urinary crystals or stones or it may have no known cause. Cats are more prone to cystitis than dogs are and it is more common in females than males. Cats with diabetes are also more prone to developing cystitis due to higher levels of glucose and protein in the urine.

Symptoms

A cat with cystitis may show some or all of these signs:

- Straining to urinate, only a few drops coming out at a time
- Frequent visits to the litter box
- Hematuria (blood in urine)
- Excessive genital licking
- Smelly urine

- Urinating outside the litter box
- Meowing when in the litter box

Treatment

The treatment for this depends on the cause. But in general, a cat's diet will usually have to be changed, water consumption should be increased by encouragement and a medication will be prescribed.

Diabetes Mellitus

What is it?

Diabetes Mellitus occurs when a cat's pancreas is unable to produce enough insulin to break down the glucose (sugar) within the body or is unable to effectively use the insulin to break down the glucose. There is no cure for Diabetes, but with the correct diet and treatment it can be managed and your cat can still live a happy life. If left untreated Diabetes can be potentially fatal to a cat. There are two types of Diabetes, these are type I and type II. Type I Diabetes means that your cat is unable to produce enough insulin and so will need to be given insulin injections for the rest of its life. Type II Diabetes means that your cat's body cannot use the insulin it produces effectively, some of these cats will require insulin injections, but some may be able to be given oral medication to control blood glucose. Diabetes is more common in overweight or senior cats.

Symptoms

A cat with diabetes may show some or all of these signs:

- Increased thirst
- Increased hunger (Early stage)
- Loss of appetite (Later stage)
- Weight loss
- Lack of energy
- Increased urination

Treatment

A diabetic cat should be fed a low-carbohydrate diet to reduce the amount of glucose in the body. Insulin will need to be administered through injection once or sometimes twice daily. There are also oral medications, but insulin injection treatment is more common. Regular blood tests will be carried out by your veterinarian to ensure your cats blood glucose levels are at the correct level, it is also possible to check blood glucose levels using home kits.

Ear Mites

What is it?

Ear mites are one of the most common health problems in cats. They are tiny insects that live in a cat's ear canal and feed by biting the skin. Ear mites can leave the ear canal and travel over the body. They are highly contagious amongst other animals as well as cats, including dogs, rabbits and ferrets; they are almost never found to go on humans. Cats of any age can get ear mites. An infected female with kittens, may infect her whole litter.

Symptoms

A cat with ear mites may show some or all of these signs:

- Scratching the ears more than usual
- Shaking the head
- Ears are flattened or laid back
- May cry in pain when ears are touched
- Foul odor coming from the ears

Treatment

The ears should be cleaned before treatment is started, as ear wax can shelter the mites from being destroyed. A medication prescribed by your veterinarian should then be administered.

Feline Herpes

What is it?

Feline herpes is an acute upper respiratory virus. It is most common in kittens and overcrowded environments, such as catteries and multi cat households. Kittens and older cats are at a greater risk than healthy cats and are also more likely to die from feline herpes. Once a cat is infected with feline herpes, it will carry it for life. The first outbreak will usually be the most severe and then it will be able to be kept in check, with only the occasional outbreak in times of stress. If a pregnant cat catches herpes, it may lead to abortion of her kittens. Humans and other animal are not able to catch feline herpes.

Symptoms

A cat with feline herpes may show some or all of these signs:

- Frequent Sneezing
- Discharge from the nose and eyes
- Eye ulcers
- Conjunctivitis or pink eye (swelling of the eyelid)
- Congestion
- Fever
- Depression
- Loss of appetite
- Drooling
- Squinting

Treatment

There is no cure for herpes, but with treatment from your veterinarian the symptoms can be cleared up.

Feline Immunodeficiency Virus (FIV)

What is it?

FIV is a similar virus to human HIV and affects the immune system, making it easier for a cat to pick up other viruses and diseases. FIV is not curable and your cat will have it for life, although it can be treated, to reduce symptoms. The most common way that FIV is transmitted from cat to cat, is through biting, this causes the infected cat's saliva to be directly passed into the un-infected cats blood stream. Transmission through groups of cats who don't fight isn't likely, but it is a good idea to keep an FIV infected cat as an only cat. The virus is most common in free-roaming outdoor cats, which fight with other cats regularly. Males are more likely to get the virus than females, as they are more territorial, especially un-neutered males. FIV cannot be transmitted to humans or other animals.

Symptoms

A cat with FIV may show some or all of these signs:

- Poor coat condition
- Persistent fever
- Loss of appetite
- Gingivitis and Stomatitis (Inflammation of the gums and mouth)
- Diarrhea
- Weight loss
- Abortion of kittens in female cats
- Seizures
- Behavior changes

Treatment

A healthy diet should be fed to your cat. Medication will be given for secondary infections; anti-inflammatory medication will be given and also immune-enhancing medication. Cats with FIV should be kept indoors to protect it from getting any diseases and also prevent it from passing the virus on to another cat. Spaying/neutering your cat will make it easier to keep it from trying to get outdoors, as un-spayed/neutered cats will want to roam to find potential mates.

Fleas

What is it?

Fleas are tiny brown insects that live in a cat's fur and feed off of the cat's blood. They may also transfer into the home and live in carpets and can bite humans. Flea bites can be extremely itchy for cats and can cause anemia, especially in kittens, which can be life threatening. Fleas are the most common external parasite and can live for 7-14 days, living their lives feeding from your cat and laying eggs within your carpets or upholstery.

Symptoms

A cat with fleas may show some or all of these signs:

- Frantic biting or scratching of the body
- Excessive grooming
- Hair loss
- Agitation

- Red skin lesions
- Muscle loss
- Pale gums
- Lethargy
- Specks on the fur/skin
- Tiny black or red/brown insects crawling in the fur

Treatments

Fleas can be treated with a number of different products such as powders, sprays, collars, spot-ons and oral tablets. You should also treat your house for fleas, there are many household spays dedicated to killing fleas. Just treating your cat isn't enough, because your cat can be infested again once the treatment wears off.

Heart Disease

What is it?

Heart disease includes a range of different heart disorders, of which some cats are born with and in others it may develop during the cat's life. Heart disease can be a cause of sudden death in young cats, which may not have shown any symptoms of disease. The most common form of heart disease in cats is cardiomyopathy and is the most common cause of heart failure. The cause of heart disease isn't always known, but some underlying causes include, hyperthyroidism (overactive thyroid), hypertension (high blood pressure) and acromegaly (excessive growth hormone production).

Symptoms

A cat with heart disease may show some or all of these signs:

- Breathing difficulties
- Shortness of breath
- Coughing
- Reduced ability to exercise
- Heart Murmur

Treatment

In some cases of heart disease, surgical correction may be possible. If the disease was caused by an underlying problem, then treating that can improve heart function and will potentially prolong life.

Hyperthyroidism

What is it?

Hyperthyroidism or overactive thyroid gland is caused by an increase in the production of hormones from the thyroid glands, which are situated in the neck. The thyroid hormones are responsible for regulating many processes within the body and when too much of these hormones are produced it creates a negative impact on the body and cats can become seriously ill. Thyroid hormones are also used to burn up energy and cats with hypertension tend to burn up their energy too quickly, resulting in weight loss, even though your cat may have an increased appetite. Hyperthyroidism is usually seen more commonly in middle aged and senior cats and is rarely seen in cats under the age of 7. Both male and female cats are equally as likely to get hyperthyroidism.

Symptoms

A cat with hyperthyroidism may show some or all of these signs:

- Weight loss
- Increased appetite
- Diarrhea
- Vomiting
- Increased thirst
- Poor skin and coat condition
- Hyperactivity

Treatment

Most cats will able to have the symptoms of hyperthyroidism completely reversed with the correct treatment. There are four main ways of treating hyperthyroidism; these are by medication, surgery to remove the affected tissue, radioactive iodine therapy or a change to the diet, which has a strictly controlled level of iodine in it.

Kidney Failure

What is it?

Kidney failure is when the kidneys are unable to remove waste products from the blood. This causes a build-up of toxic waste which can lead to kidney disease. Kidney failure can come on acutely or occur gradually over a period of time, usually weeks or months. Kidney failure is a leading cause of death in domestic cats and is most common in middle aged to senior cats.

Symptoms

A cat with kidney disease may show some or all of these signs:

- Loss of appetite
- Increase thirst
- Increased urination or no urination
- Vomiting
- Diarrhea
- Depression
- Weight loss
- Bad breath
- Sore mouth
- Weakness and lack of energy

Treatment

If kidney failure is detected early, then using treatment can help slow the process and prolong your cat's life.

Liver Disease

What is it?

Liver disease arises when the liver is damaged, resulting in loss of function. It can be chronic (slow and progressive) or acute (sudden onset). There are several causes of liver disease in cats which include anorexia, damage from toxins, cancer and inflammatory disorders of the liver. Cats of all ages can get liver disease, but it is most common in middle aged to senior cats.

Symptoms

A cat with liver disease may show some or all of these signs:

- Loss of appetite
- Weight loss
- Jaundice (yellowing of the gums, skin or whites of eyes)
- Increased thirst
- Changes in behavior
- Lack of energy
- Depression
- Excessive drooling

Treatment

The treatment for liver disease depends on the cause. This can include surgery, a change of diet or medication. The quicker liver disease is diagnosed and treated, the better chance your cat has at survival.

Lyme Disease

What is it?

Lyme disease is transmitted through ticks which attach themselves to your pet. Ticks are small parasites, which feed on your cat's blood. Lyme disease is caused by bacteria and causes inflammation of the joints, which can lead to lameness. The disease doesn't usually occur, unless the tick has been attached to your cat for more than 18 hours. Lyme disease is most common in outdoor cats who live in rural, woodland areas.

Symptoms

A cat with Lyme disease may show some or all of these signs:

- Lethargy
- Loss of appetite
- Reluctance to jump or climb stairs
- Limping, or reluctance to put weight on paws

Treatment

Lyme disease will usually be treated on an outpatient basis, unless the symptoms are severe. It will usually be treated with a course of antibiotics and you should keep your cat indoors. The treatment period will usually last around 4 weeks. The symptoms of Lyme disease may not always be completely resolved in some cats and long-term joint pain may continue, even after the bacteria have been destroyed from your cat's system.

Ringworm

What is it?

Although the name suggests otherwise, ringworm isn't actually a worm – but a fungus. It can affect the skin, hair and nails and is highly contagious. It is able to spread to other animals in the house and humans too. A cat can get ringworm from direct contact with an infected animal or through contact with bedding, dishes or other materials which have been contaminated with the skin cells or hairs of infected animals. Ringworm spores are very hardy and can survive in the environment for as long as a year. Any cat is able to develop ringworm, but it is most common in kittens and cats with longer hair. Ringworm can spread very quickly in crowded environments such as catteries and multi-cat households.

Symptoms

Some cats with ringworm show no symptoms, but they may show some or all of the following signs:

- Flaky skin
- Skin lesions which usually appear on the head, ears and forelimbs
- Bald patches
- Redness of the skin

Treatment

Treatment for ringworm varies depending on the severity of the case. You may be prescribed a shampoo or ointment which contains medication to kill the fungus. In some cases, oral medication may be needed. Treatment may last for several months to ensure the fungus has been completely killed. It is also important that the cat's environment is treated, to prevent to infection from recurring. If you have a multi-pet household, it is a good idea to quarantine the infected pet from the other pets.

Roundworm

What is it?

They are the most common worm parasite in cats. Roundworms can live in the stomach and intestines and may grow up to 5 inches in length. Roundworm eggs are extremely hardy and can live for several months in soil. Cats can pass on roundworms to other cats through contact with infected stool or a female cat can pass larvae to her kittens through her milk. Cats can also acquire roundworm by ingesting the eggs from contact with soil containing the eggs and licking it from their body, or by eating a host animal such as a beetle or a rodent. Roundworm is most common in kittens.

Symptoms

A cat with roundworm may show some or all of these signs:

- Weight loss or failure to gain weight
- Dull coat
- Pot-bellied appearance
- Diarrhea
- Kittens may vomit up roundworms or pass them in feces

Treatment

A de-wormer can be used; these come in oral tablet form or as an oral paste. Many veterinarians suggest de-worming kittens monthly until the age of 6 months, whether they are infected or not.

Tapeworm

What is it?

Tapeworm is the most common internal parasite in adult cats. Tapeworms live in a cat's intestines and can range from 1inch up to several feet in length. To completely eliminate a tapeworm infestation, the head of the tapeworm must be destroyed; otherwise, the worm will be able to regenerate. The body segments of the tapeworm which contain the eggs will be passed in the feces. Tapeworms are transmitted by fleas or lice, which harbor immature tapeworms in their intestines. They can also be transmitted through a cat eating rodents, uncooked meat or raw freshwater fish. Tapeworm can occur in any cat, but is most common in adults.

Symptoms

A cat with tape worm may show some or all of these signs:

- White/cream-colored pieces in the feces
- White/cream-colored pieces stuck around the anus
- Increased licking/biting of the anus
- Rubbing or dragging the anus across the floor due to itching

Treatment

A de-wormer specifically for tapeworm should be given to the infected cat. If the tapeworms were transmitted from fleas, then deworming should be combined with a flea treatment.

Cat Breath

Here, we are going to talk about getting rid of your Birman cat's bad breath.

Bad breath, known as halitosis can be caused by a variety of things including bacteria build up and some health issues so while you do not expect your cat's breath to be minty fresh, it would be nice if when they give you a sweet little nose rub that their breath doesn't discomfort you. Bad breath in cats and humans are both caused by bacteria found in the mouth. Diet and dermatological issues could be the cause for your feline friend's bad breath.

If your cat's bad breath is persistent for a long period of time, then it could be an indication of a serious medical problems such as; abnormalities in the mouth, respiratory system, gastrointestinal tract, liver or kidneys. Mostly, the odor producing bacteria that causes bad breath in cats is normally caused by plaque and tartar buildup around the teeth and tartar being the coating of bacteria, food, and minerals seen on your cat's teeth close to the gum line normally yellow in color.

To cure your cat's bad breath, you'll need to get rid of the buildup of tartar. Most cat foods out there that are designed to reduce the buildup of tartar, many containing enzymes that will literally dissolve it. Some crunchy cat treats also helps to eliminate and prevent tartar. If the buildup of tartar is very bad then you may need to have your cat's teeth professionally cleaned. Once the tartar has been removed, the bad breath should disappear immediately.

You may be able to clean the tartar off your cat's teeth at home too as there are several toothpastes available for cats in a variety of different flavors and a toothbrush. Battery-operated spin brushes works great if your cat will tolerate it because the motion helps remove tartar buildup. Look for a toothpaste that contains enzymes that will dissolve tartar and help cure bad breath. If you start brushing your cat's teeth at a young age, you can virtually eliminate any type of tartar buildup that will ultimately lead to bad breath completely.

Bacteria that lead to tartar buildup can often be found in your cat's diet therefore you should always look for high-quality foods to keep them healthy. You will also want to avoid feeding them raw meats and canned foods that have been left out for a long period of time. A good rule of thumb with canned cat food is to discard any leftovers your cat leaves behind after 30 minutes as it will help reduce the risk of them consuming unwanted bacteria and help reduce the effects of bad breath.

When you out shopping for treats for your favorite feline friend, make sure that you look for treats that are designed to help with tartar. Just as humans, it is not a good idea to brush your cat's teeth after they have finished eating meal as it helps get the bacteria out of their mouth before it has time to build up on their teeth.

As mentioned earlier, if your cat's bad breath persist, it may not be because of tartar build up but could be either a liver or kidney disease so If you notice that their bad breath isn't going away after brushing and removing tartar then you should take your cat to the vet for checkup immediately because though it may be something simple, it is always better to be safe than sorry. Your veterinarian can pinpoint the problem and let you know what the cause is and how you should treat it.

Stress

You may not understand exactly what is causing your cat to be stressed, but you can watch for signs that your cat is stressed. When a cat suddenly becomes aggressive towards people and other pets, goes to the bathroom outside of the litter box, marks or sprays in the house, hides from those in the household, or begins losing their hair you can be assured the cat is struggling to deal with the stress they are facing.

If you notice these symptoms in your cat, you need to first make an appointment with your veterinarian to ensure that the problem is stress and not something more severe.

If your cat is struggling with stress, you need to assess the environment your cat is living in. First, you need to recognize if there is a lot of yelling or loud noises in the home. Cats prefer a calm environment and loud noises can cause them to become overly stressed.

Next, you need to make sure your cat has a place it can go to in order to get away from other animals in the house as well as people. Cats do not like to be held all the time; they do not need company all the time and they like to have time alone. If your cat does not have a place it can go to enjoy some solitude you may begin seeing symptoms of stress.

You may also not have enough litter boxes in the home. Often times sharing, a litter box will cause a cat to not want to use it or cause the cat to feel stressed. At the most, you should only have two cats sharing a litter box. If you can provide one box per cat that is even better.

If you have more than one cat in the house, make sure you are offering each of them food in a separate area of the house so they are able to eat their food in peace and without being bullied or having their food taken away by a bigger cat.

Make sure the cat is getting enough stimulation with toys, playing and make sure they are able to look outside when they want. Most cats will spend hours just staring out a window if they have access to one.

Make sure the cat has a place it can climb to. Cats like to be up high, it makes them feel safe, so if you want to reduce the stress your cat is dealing with make sure to get them something they can climb on.

Finally, you need to keep the changes in your cat's life to a minimum. If change is a must, make sure it is gradual so the cat does not become overly stressed.

Chapter Eight: Showing Your Birman Cat

Generally, people who breed Birman cats are also the ones who show them. Breeders are, after all, hardcore enthusiasts.

Cat shows allow them to display their animals and the excellence of their bloodlines, and an impressive list of awards lends prestige to a cattery.

This is not to say that an individual who owns a beautiful Birman may not want to show that cat, but most exhibitors are also breeders.

This is one of the reasons cat shows are such an excellent resource for people who are considering adopting a purebred cat. You won't walk out of a show with a kitten, but you can certainly walk out with a fistful of business cards.

For this reason alone, you may find yourself in the cat show environment as a spectator, and it's imperative that you understand how to behave yourself!

The Dos and Don'ts of Attending a Cat Show

Spectators at cat shows have to remember the cardinal rule. DON'T TOUCH!

That's hard to do when you're among so many beautiful animals. Try to remember that this rule is not to penalize you, but to protect the cats.

Most cat diseases are highly communicable. If you pet a cat infected with a disease and touch another cat, you've just passed along the bacteria or virus.

If you are asked to pet a cat at a show, consider it a high compliment and don't blink when the exhibitor hands you a bottle of hand sanitizer. Use it, and then enjoy the rare chance to interact with the cat.

If someone shouts, "Right of way," yield. Move. Get out of the way. Or get run over! Cat shows are amazingly hectic, crowded, and busy places. When exhibitors are called to the ring, they have to get there in a limited amount of time or face disqualification.

Understand that if you're talking to an exhibitor who gets called to the ring, they will likely turn on their heel, take their cats, and leave without so much as a word. They are trusting you to know the ropes and understand that they aren't being rude. They're in a hurry.

If you are near the show ring when judging starts, stop talking and LISTEN. You do not want to do anything to distract the exhibitor or worse yet the cat, and, because judge make comments on animals while they are examining them, you'll likely learn a great deal by paying close attention.

Finally, if you hear the dreaded alarm, "LOOSE CAT," your only response should be to FREEZE. You should never try to help. Be quiet, be still, and do nothing more than signal the location of the outlaw animal should you see it.

The Mechanics of Cat Shows in Action

Cat shows are different from dog shows in a number of ways. Cats are only removed from their cages while being judged, otherwise they're kept secured at all other times.

The atmosphere is very hectic, and almost festive, with exhibitors elaborately decorating their cages and the adjacent area. In spite of all the activity, however, the actual progress of the show can be agonizingly slow.

Cats are far less receptive to being judged, and many categorically do not like the show atmosphere. Dramatic escapes are a panicked hallmark of these events.

Also, unlike dog shows, there will be a class for household pets, which is often a prime attraction for young people to become interested in the cat fancy.

The actual evaluation of the animals is done according to published breed standards formulated by the official body sponsoring the show.

The more completely an animal conforms to the points of the breed standard, the higher its score and performance in the ring.

All governing bodies have slightly different rules for how shows are administered. Details are available on the homepage of the given official body.

Examples include:

- The International Cat Association
- Fédération Internationale Féline
- World Cat Federation
- Cat Fanciers Association
- Feline Federation Europe
- Australia Cat Federation
- American Association of Cat Enthusiasts
- American Cat Fanciers Association

Traveling with Your Birman Cat

Traveling with a cat can be challenging, especially if you are driving in a vehicle. Most cats are not fond of being in a moving vehicle, unless they have been taught to get used to it from a young age or they are an extraordinary cat.

Even though you may try to acclimate your cat to riding in a car when they are young, some cats never get used to it and do not enjoy the experience.

Unless your Birman cat has been trained to ride in a car, and likes the experience, you should always put your cat in a sturdy cat carrier when you go to the vet or on a trip. While you can use a soft-sided carrier, they are really made for airplane travel and it is better to use a hard-sided carrier when you're in a car.

The sturdier carrier gives them a bit more room to move around, especially as they are a bigger breed of cat, but it can also help protect your cat in case of an accident.

If you are traveling a short distance, such as to the vet, you may not need to make any extra preparations for your cat. However, if you are taking them on a longer trip, you will need to take some cat essentials along.

Traveling with a pet is much like traveling with a child, you need to take some supplies in order to make the trip more comfortable for them by keeping them calm.

Line their carrier with a blanket or a towel to give them something soft to cuddle up in, especially if you are traveling during the cooler months. A Birman cat can easily withstand cold weather, but they would still like to have something soft on which to lie.

Take water, food, bowls, a litter pan and litter on the trip to accommodate their needs. Place their favorite small toys in the carrier with them for both comfort and to give them something to pass the time.

The best place to put the carrier is in the middle of the back seat. This placement will prevent the sun from shining directly onto the carrier, which can make the trip uncomfortably warm for your Birman cat.

Secure the carrier with a seatbelt to keep it from sliding around on the seat in case you have to make a sudden stop or swerve the car. If the carrier isn't secure, your cat can be injured if the carrier overturns.

Some cats have motion sickness and it can be worsened if they can see outside during the trip. To help prevent their motion sickness, place their carrier on the floorboard behind one of the front seats. Try to prevent the floor air blower from directly blowing onto the carrier, especially if you have the heater on because it can get too hot for a thick furred Birman cat.

On a longer trip, you should set up a litter box inside of your vehicle. A covered litter pan works best because it will prevent the litter from spilling onto the floor of your vehicle.

Unlike dogs, your cat doesn't need to stretch its legs on a trip until you stop for the night. It is important that you keep your cat in its carrier while traveling, especially when you stop so that it doesn't bolt out of the car and get lost in unfamiliar territory.

Traveling on an airplane has its own unique issues for you and your pet. Before you take them with you on a plane, you need to contact the airline to find out their pet policy before purchasing a ticket. Although it is faster to look for their policy on their website, policies are subject to change and you may wish to contact them directly to confirm the information on their site. Most airlines allow pets to be carried on the plane, which is what you should do with your cat.

A soft-sided pet carrier will fit under the seat in front of you, but you can also buy the seat beside you and place a hard-sided carrier on it. As you would when traveling by car, take some things with you to help comfort them. Place a blanket and their favorite toy in the carrier with them so they can snuggle while traveling.

You will need to get a health certificate from your cat's vet before traveling by plane. The airline will want to see that your cat has been vaccinated before you can take it on the plane. Keep the health certificate with you at all times so it is easily accessible. Put a collar on your cat with an identification tag with his or her name, your telephone number and address in case your cat manages to escape the carrier.

If you are traveling internationally on vacation, it would be better to have a trusted friend or family member look after your cat while you're away than it would be to try to take your cat with you.

Unless you are moving to another country, making arrangements for a pet can be a hassle on short international trips. Some countries will not allow foreign animals into their country, while other countries require them to be quarantined on arrival. It can take weeks, if not months, to get approval to take your pet into another country.

Some cats may require a visit to their vet before you take your trip. Some of them need to be sedated because they do not travel well due to car or air-sickness. Always check with your veterinarian before giving your cat anything to keep it calm.

Some sedatives or tranquilizers will affect cat's body temperature or they may have other adverse reactions to them, even if they are made from natural herbs. It is better to let your vet sedate them or advise you on which sedative is best for your cat.

By being properly prepared and by taking the supplies your cat needs along on the trip, you can enjoy traveling with your cat. Work with your Birman cat to train them to lie calmly in a carrier so they will be used to it when it is time to take them on a trip. Start with small car rides across town and gradually make them longer so your cat will get used to car travel. They may never like it, but with patience and preparation, the travel experience will be better for you and your cat.

Chapter Nine: Breeding Your Birman Cat

Here, we are going to go over some of the things you should know before breeding your Birman cat.

The population of cats is the United States alone will surprise you and nearly all experts will tell you that it better you spay your cat instead of breeding it but no matter what the experts say, a lot of people still want to have a litter of kittens from their beloved feline friend but before you decide to breed your cat, you should think about a few things first. First of all, breeding your cats is not as simple as it sounds. You will have to be in charge of safeguarding the health of your cat and her kittens and will need to be ready to handle any situation that will occur along the way.

Here are a few things to consider before breeding your cat:

1- Do you have plenty of time to dedicate to your cat and her kittens?
2- Do you have enough money set aside for basic vet costs and unexpected emergences?
3- Do you have adequate space for mother cat and up to half a dozen little bundles of joy?
4- If you can't find homes for all of the new kittens are you prepared to keep them?

Having a litter of kittens takes a lot of time, not only from the mother cat, but from you too as well. You will have to be prepared to commit at least two months of continuous care to mother cat and her little bundles of joy after the litter is born.

You will be responsible for:

1- Making sure that mother cat is well-nourished.
2- Cleaning up the area that the kittens are in on a daily basis.
3- Watching over the kittens and keeping an eye on their development.
4- Taking them to the vet for their first shots and more.

Breeding cats will also require a good bit of space. If you have a small apartment, you will have to plan carefully and should also make sure that your family is on board with the idea so that you will have plenty of help to lighten up your load bearing in mind that, kittens are curious and once they become more active it will be hard to keep them contained. When it comes to breeding your Birman cat you should always have a plan, including how you intend to care for them, where you were going to keep them and how you are going to find homes for the kittens that you aren't planning to keep.

Do not forget that things do change- someone who wanted a kitten may change their mind once the litter is born hence make room for some of these unforeseen as to whether or not you can keep these kittens all by yourself. You will also want to educate yourself a bit on some basic breeding procedures. You'll need to know what to feed your pregnant cat because their diets are very important for the development of the kittens and will also want to be prepared for what takes place during birth as far as any problems you may encounter along the way from cutting umbilical cords to delivering early, you'll need to be very well prepared.

If you do not live close to a veterinarian, you should have the necessary supplies handy and must know how to handle things in the event of a c- section - these is rare, but again it is always better to be safe than sorry. Raising a litter of kittens will definitely require extra funds as well. The vet bills can get expensive and even if you go through the entire pregnancy without going to the vet, you'll still need some de-worming and vaccinations for the kittens before they can go to their new homes. You will also need to consider the cost of food because even though mother cat will be nursing the kittens for the first eight weeks you can start introducing them to food when they are around four weeks old which means your food bill is going to increase substantially. Once you have decided to take the plunge into breeding you must be sure to arm yourself with the proper knowledge and supplies needed, so that you will be ready to take on the job squarely when the time comes.

Who is a Breeder?

Basically, a breeder is one who is engaged in the business of carefully mating selected animals to reproduce offspring that exhibit specific qualities and characteristics unique to a breed. Becoming a Birman cat breeder therefore involves breeding pure-bred Birman cats with the aim of reproducing kittens that exhibit qualities and characteristics unique to the breed. You can become a breeder purely for fun as a hobby, to promote the breed or as a business. Whether you choose to breed as a hobby or as a business, you will have a good opportunity to participate in professional cat shows and competitions. Becoming a breeder does not require that you must have attained a specific level of education. You must however demonstrate that you have compassion and a genuine interest in the Birman cat breed.

Things to Note

Although you may have compassion and interest in the Birman cat breed to a point where you want to become a breeder, there are important things you need to take note of. From the onset, becoming a Birman cat breeder will not make you rich overnight. Becoming a breeder can be very expensive and you should not expect to recoup your expenses within a short period. You need to start breeding as a hobby before you can expect to start receiving some income. Indeed, most current successful Birman cat breeders started off breeding as a hobby before graduating to full time commercial breeders.

The second thing to note is that the practice of breeding requires commitment, devotion and time. Time in particular is very important. It becomes very necessary that you devote most of your time to your cattery. This is because the cattery requires daily cleaning, feeding, grooming and treatment of your cats. This is the only way you will be able to breed healthy Birman cats that will encourage many in your neighborhood to buy.

Third, becoming a breeder requires some level of financial investment. You will need to construct a cattery at a suitable location, install the necessary infrastructure, buy cat food and engage the service of a vet among other costs. You will also need to incur other expenses in having your cats registered by relevant bodies and pay some fee to your local authority. Most current Birman cat breeders stated off with only two cats in small rooms right within their homes, something that you too may consider.

Lastly, you need to be prepared to handle the emotional toll that comes along with the practice of breeding. The fact that you will be taking care of many cats and mating them means that they will be giving birth. It is common for some pregnant cats to die when giving birth in catteries. Others will die of natural causes including diseases. Kittens will also be at risk of dying of natural causes. Watching as your lovely Birman cats and kittens die will take a serious toll on your mind.

Where to Start

The best way to start off as a breeder is to prepare a room in your home to serve as your cattery on a temporary basis. This is not only cost effective; it will also be easy to manage your cats. Such preparation involves equipping the room with all the necessary equipment and supplies your cats will need to survive. These include food, water/food dishes, scratch post, bed and beddings and cat play toys among other equipment and supplies. You also need to engage the service of a veterinarian who will be responsible for treating your cats whenever they fall sick, get injured and in giving vaccinations.

The second step to becoming a Birman cat breeder is identifying an established breeder to buy kittens or cats from. It is mandatory that you buy from an established and registered breeder. This is because such a breeder will be breeding pedigree Birman cats that are properly registered.

You have the option of buying a female Birman cat (queen), in which case you will be obligated to buy a male (tom) afterwards or take the queen to a vet or breeder for insemination. You also have the option of buying two Birman cats; a tom and a queen. Depending on your preference and level of preparedness in becoming a breeder, you may choose to buy kittens or adult cats.

The fourth step to becoming a breeder is to register as a breeder. You have several options on how to register, depending on your location and preference. There are both national and international cat registries from which you can choose one to register with. International cat registries include UK's Cat Fanciers Association (CFA), France's Federation Internationale Feline (FIFe), UAE's Emirates Feline Federation (EFF), The American Cat Fanciers Association (ACFA) and The International Cat Association (TICA). National cat registries include UK's Governing Council of the Cat Fancy (GCCF), UK's Felis Britannica (member of FIFe), PRC's Cat Aficionado Association (CAA) and the Canadian Cat Association (CCA) among other national registries.

Registering your cats provides for several benefits. First, you will be recognized as a registered breeder licensed to breed Birman cats. Secondly, you will have the opportunity to participate in both national and international cat shows and have your cats participate in different championships depending on their age. Participation in such championships can earn you good money depending on how your cats perform.

Thirdly, you will have the opportunity to learn better breeding techniques both from a registry you register with and other Birman cat breeders. Registering as a breeder also gives you the opportunity to know the exact breed standards you will have to maintain as a Birman cat breeder. Lastly, you will have the opportunity to be appointed as a Birman cat show judge after gaining reasonable breeding experience if you so wish. Note that you can register with more than one registry if you so wish so long as you are financially capable of meeting all registration fees.

Different cat registries do organize different Birman cat shows and competitions. CFA for example organizes the Kitten Shows and Championships (for pedigreed kittens aged between one and three years), Championships (for unaltered cats aged eight months), Premiership (for altered cats aged above two year), Veteran (for both altered and unaltered cats aged seven years) and Household (for non-pedigreed cats aged two years months).

General Breeding Information

Successful registration as a Birman cat breeder is just the first step to becoming a professional breeder. Because the cats you buy will have been registered by their breeder, you will need to register the litter that your cats give birth to. This you will do with the registry you registered with. Registering your litter entitles you to a unique prefix that will hence forth be used as the first name for all the litter that your cats will produce. It will be your responsibility to indicate a prefix you will wish to use.

Different cat registries have different requirements when registering prefixes. The GCCF for example requires that you must have been registered as a breeder for at least one year before you can register your litter.

Unlike some cat breeds that take up to two years to become sexually active, Birman cats become sexually mature reasonably fast.

Both your tom and queen become sexually active with the queen capable of attaining pregnancy when it is between one and two years. You will be able to know when your queen is on heat when it becomes too vocal and lies on the floor as if presenting itself to a male.

Your queen's gestation period is between 60 and 65 days. The last week of pregnancy will see your queen look for the most appropriate place to give birth. It will look for a dark yet safe place where to give forth its litter. Birman cats generally give birth to average litters, between three and five litters.

Building a Cattery

It is only appropriate that you build a cattery once you have established yourself as a Birman cat breeder. A cattery is where you house your cats for commercial purpose. Although yours will be a breeding cattery, you will also have the option of using it as a boarding cattery in which case other cat owners not able to travel with their cats will bring their cats to you for safe keeping at a fee.

It is mandatory that you apply for a license from your local authority before you can build a cattery. You also need to follow cattery building guidelines provided by the registry you register with. Every registry has minimum cattery construction requirements that you must stick to before you can receive another license from the registrar. A registrar will only grant you a cattery license after inspecting your cattery and certifying it to have met the set minimum construction requirements. Most registrars engage the service of local veterinarians to undertake search inspections. It will be the responsibility of the appointed vet to inspect your cattery on a regular basis to ensure that you stick to set breeding guidelines.

There are several minimum requirements when it comes to constructing a cattery, one of which is space. Your cattery needs to be spacious enough to accommodate all your cats comfortably. The minimum space per cat is set at 30 cubic feet. In addition, you need to create a space for play, grooming and maintenance. Established breeders do go the extra mile to group and house their stock according to their age. Groups that are housed in separated cages is one way of preventing diseases.

The other very important minimum requirement you need to meet is to construct your cattery in such a way that it allows for free flow of fresh air for your cats' good health. Your cattery should not only have enough windows but large enough windows that allow for free flow of air in and out of the cattery. The fact that Birman cats are both indoor and outdoor pets make it necessary that you have windows that allow sufficient amount of light into the cattery. Artificial lighting may be necessary to achieve this if the windows do not provide for sufficient natural light.

Cat registrars are very strict when it comes to cattery sanitation. Not only are you required to construct your cattery in a clean environment; you will also need to ensure that there is a high standard of cleanliness in and around your cattery on a daily basis. Sanitation is one of the most important things that an appointed veterinarian will always pay attention to whenever he/she pays a visit to your cattery.

Such guidelines are not only requirements; they are mandatory taking into account the fact that failure to observe the same can lead to occurrence of cat diseases that can wipe out your cat population. Apart from such guidelines, you will need to have all the necessary supplies and equipment that your cats will need for good health and play activities. You will also need to engage the service of a veterinarian who will be available whenever situation demand and when it is time for vaccinations.

Where to Find Buyers

Selling of pets is now a booming business across the world. This is very evident in the number of pet breeders established. It is a fact that more homeowners and families are starting to appreciate pets and they go to extra miles to ensure that they have one or two in their homes.

Of all pets, cats happen to be appreciated by homeowners and individual families. This is simply because of health benefits associated with living with cats, benefits that homeowners and individual families have come to appreciate.

It is therefore apparent that you will never fail to find a buyer for your Birman kittens should you choose to start a Birman cat breeding program. Even so, you will still need to market your kittens just like you would with selling any other commodity.

Your first point of marketing should obviously be your friends and colleagues. These are the people most likely to buy your kittens. These are also the group of people who can promote your cattery by word of mouth to their friends, colleagues and members of your local community.

Apart from friends and colleagues, your local community is no doubt the next category of people you will need to market your Birman kittens to. Making your cattery known to your local community is very important considering the fact that community members will be able to promote your business to a wider population.

You will also be able to easily find buyers for your Birman kittens if you have a strong online presence. It will be necessary to have a well-designed cattery website. Not only will you be able to sell your kittens to customers at your local level but countrywide and across the world as well.

One area you will need to have a strong presence on is on social media networks. The fact that social media networks have become a huge market place makes it necessary that you also expose your cattery to users of social media networks.

It is important to point out that it will be beneficial to you to register with both national and international Birman cat associations and clubs. This is because these associations and clubs are always the first point of call for Birman cat lovers looking for information on reputable Birman cat breeders to buy kittens from.

Final Thoughts on Breeding and Showing Birman Cats

Always remember that the idea of breeding and/or showing Birman cats may, in the end, prove more attractive and "doable" than the reality.

You can very happily have Birman cats in your life without running a cattery or ever showing a cat in the ring.

The only valid reason to become a breeder is love of the breed and a desire to improve its genetics. Breeding is a hobby, but it's also a way of life. Don't take it on lightly.

As for showing cats, although many people enjoy the process, and cat shows enhance many lives, it's really not a natural environment for a cat.

Birman cats are adaptable, and cope reasonably well with being shown, but for many breeds, the stresses far outweigh any potential benefits.

Before you make a decision to breed or to show Birman cats, learn everything you can about the cats themselves, and about everything that is involved with either activity.

These are not simple decisions and they should not be made on the spur of the moment or without full consideration for your welfare, but especially for that of your cat or cats.

Conclusion

Cats, Birman cats in particular, make very good pets. You will never feel bored when living with a Birman cat. It is a playful and lively cat that engages you all the time. It will always want you to give it attention, which is perfectly normal since it may be the only trusted companion you can have at home.

The Birman is one cat that does not discriminate when it comes to family members. It is very good with children to who it develops a very strong bond because of its playful and calm nature. Furthermore, the cat is very receptive to training.

According to research studies published in the Journal of Vascular and Interventional Neurology, living with a cat provides for several health benefits. One of the main benefits is that living with a cat reduces the risk of suffering from cardiovascular diseases including heart attack. Other health benefits associated with living with a cat include reduced risk of high stress level, reduced cholesterol level and reduced risk of depression.

Children raised in an environment where there is a cat have also been noted to grow up healthier than those raised in an environment where there is none. Unlike most cat breeds, the Birman breed is very cost effective so long as you give it proper care. It is generally a healthy breed that is less vulnerable to common diseases that other cat breeds are highly vulnerable to. The fact that the breed's kittens do not inherit serious diseases/health conditions translates into reduced veterinary expenses.

The popularity of the Birman across the globe is not in doubt. It is one of the cat breeds that is gaining popularity at an unprecedented rate. Its' growing popularity is indeed evident in the increasing number of Birman cat breeders registering with different cat registries around the world. It is also not surprising that dedicated Birman cat clubs are also being established in different regions around the world.

You can choose to have two Birman cats as indoor pets or join the big league as a Birman cat breeder. While you will have a cat that is loyal, obedient and a valuable companion if you choose to have them as pets, you are also most likely to excel as a breeder should you decide to become a Birman cat breeder.

Glossary of Cat Terms

Ailurophile- A person who loves cats.

Ailurophobe - A person who fears or even hates cat.

Allergen - In relation to cats, the primary allergen, the substance that causes an allergic reaction in some people, is, Fel d 1, a protein produced by the cat's sebaceous glands, and present in its saliva.

Allergy - A high level of sensitivity present in some people to a given substance, like the protein Fel d 1 in cats. Generally, the reaction includes, but is not limited to watering eyes, sneezing, itching, and skin rashes.

Alter - A term which refers to the neutering or spaying of a cat or dog.

Bloodline - The verifiable line of descent that establishes an animal's pedigree.

Breed Standard - A set of standards for a given breed formulated by parent breed clubs and used as the basis for evaluating show quality animals.

Breed - Term that refers to a group of cats with defined physical characteristics that are related by common ancestry.

Breeder - A person who works with a particular breed of cats, producing offspring from high-quality dams and sires for the purpose of maintaining and improving the genetic quality of the line.

Breeding - The process in which dams and sires are paired for the purpose of producing offspring.

Breeding Program - An organized and ongoing program in which cats are mated selectively to produce offspring that are ideal examples of the breed.

Breeding Quality - A term describing a cat that meets the standards of a given breed to a degree sufficient to be included in a breeding program.

Breed True - The phrase which describes the capacity of a male and female cat to produce kittens that closely resemble themselves in accepted elements of the breed standard.

Carpal Pads - Located on a cat's front legs at the "wrists," these pads provide added traction for the animal's gait. **Castrate** - The medical procedure whereby a male cat's testicles are removed.

Caterwaul - A feline vocalization that produces a discordant, shrill sound.

Cat Fancy - Term used to describe the overall group of registered associations clubs, and individuals that breed and show cats.

Catnip - A member of the mint family, this aromatic perennial herb (Nepeta cataria) contains an oil to which some cats are strongly attracted and to which they respond with a kind of "stoned" intoxication. Kittens cannot respond to catnip until they are 8-9 months of age.

Cattery - Any establishment that exists for the purpose of housing cats, and where they are bred as part of an organized program.

Certified Pedigree - A pedigree that has been issued in an official capacity by a feline registering association.

Clowder - A collective term for a group of cats.

Coat - Term referring to a cat's fur.

Crate - Container used to safely transport cats from one location to another or to confine them temporarily for their own safety.

Crepuscular - Although known in popular lore as nocturnal animals, cats are actually crepuscular, meaning they are most active at dusk and dawn.

Crossbred - A cat that is the product of breeding a sire and a dam of different breeds.

Dam -The female in a parenting set of cats.

Dander - The small scale of hair and skin that are shed by an animal. Often responsible for allergic reactions in individuals with a sensitivity to the substance.

Declawing - A highly controversial surgical procedure that removes   a   cat's   claws   permanently.

Desex - Describes the alteration of an animal by neutering or spaying.

Domesticated - Animals that have been tamed to live with or work with humans, or that have chosen to cultivate such a relationship.

Ear Mites - Microscopic parasites that feed on the lining of a cat's ear canal, causing debris to build up, generating a foul odor, and resulting in extreme itching.

Entire - A term describing a cat that has an intact reproductive system.

Exhibitor - An individual that participates in organized cat shows.

Fel d 1 - A protein produced by the cat's sebaceous glands, and present in its saliva, which causes an allergic reaction in some people.

Feline - A member of the family Felidae. Includes lions, tigers, jaguars, and wild and domestic cats.

Fleas - Various bloodsucking insects of the order Siphonaptera. They are wingless, and their legs are adapted for jumping. They are parasitical, and feed off warm-blooded animals.

Flehmening/Flehmen Reaction - A facial gesture in cats that is often mistaken for a grimace. In reality, the cat is drawing in air to pass it over a special structure in the roof of the mouth called the Jacobsen's Organ, which functions as a second set of nostrils and allows cats to "taste" a scent.

Gene pool - In a population of organisms, the "gene pool" is the collective genetic information relative to reproduction.

Genes - Determine particular characteristics in a given organism. They are a distinct hereditary unit and consist of a DNA sequence occupying a specific location on a chromosome.

Genetic - Refers to any trait, characteristic, tendency, or condition that is inherited.

Genetically Linked Defects - Health specific problems or those relative to temperament that are passed from one generation to the next.

Genetics - The scientific study of heredity.

Genotype - Refers to the genetic makeup of an organism or a group of organisms.

Groom - The act of caring for the coat of a feline, which may include brushing, combing, trimming, or washing.

Guard Hair - Long, coarse hairs that form the outer layer of a cat's coat.

Heat - The seasonal estrus cycle of a female cat (or any other mammal).

Hereditary - Any characteristic, trait, disease, or condition that can be genetically transmitted from parent to offspring. Histamine - A physiologically active amine in plant and animal tissue released from mast cells as part of an allergic reaction in humans.

Hock - Anatomical term describing the ankle of a cat's hind leg.

Household Pet - A cat not registered to be exhibited or shown in competition.

Housetraining - The process whereby a cat is trained to use a litter box to live cleanly in a house.

Humane Societies - Any one of a number of groups that work to put an end to animal suffering due to overt acts of cruelty and other impoverishing or harmful circumstances.

Immunization - The use of inoculations to create immunity against disease. Also referred to as vaccination.

Innate - A quality, trait, or tendency present at birth and thus inborn

Inbreeding - When two closely-related cats of the same breed are mated.

Instinct - A pattern of behavior in a species that is inborn and comes in response to specific environmental stimuli. Intact - Animals that are intact possess their complete reproductive system. They have not been neutered or spayed.

Jacobsen's Organ - An organ located in the roof of a cat's mouth that allows it to "taste" a scent. Appears as two small openings and is regarded as a second set of "nostrils."

Kindle - A collective term for a group of kittens. An alternate term is "chowder."

Kitten - Young cats under the age of 6 months.

Lactation - Process by which the mammary glands form and secrete milk.

Lactating - Term used for a mammalian mother when she is secreting or producing milk.

Litter - The number of offspring in a single birth. Generally 3-4 in cats, although 6-10 is not uncommon.

Litter Box - A container filled with commercial kitty litter or sand and used in the home as a sanitary and manageable location for a cat to urinate and defecate.

Longhair - Cats with varying lengths of long hair, typically with plumed tails and prominent neck ruffs.

Mites - Small arachnids (of the order Acarina) that are parasites on animals and plants. Often seen in the ears of felines.

Moggy - The term for a mixed breed cat in the United Kingdom.

Muzzle - In cats, the part of the head projecting forward including the mouth, nose, and jaws. May also be referred to as the snout.

Neuter - The term used to describe castrating a male cat.

Nictitating Membrane - A cat's third eyelid, which is a transparent inner eyelid that serves to protect and moisten the eye.

Nocturnal - Term used to describe animals that are most active at night. It is mistakenly applied to cats, who are actually crepuscular, being most active at dawn and dusk.

Odd-Eyed - Eyes of two different colors presenting in a single individual.

Papers - The documentation of a cat's pedigree and registration.

Pedigree - A cat's genealogy presented in writing and spanning three or more generations.

Pet Quality - A cat that does not sufficiently meet the accepted standard for its breed to be shown in competition or to be used in a breeding program.

Queen - An intact female cat, one that has not been spayed.

Quick - The vascular portion of a cat's claw that will, if clipped, bleed profusely.

Rabies - A viral disease that is highly infections and typically fatal to warm blooded animals. It attacks the central nervous system and is transmitted by the bite of an infected animal.

Recognition - The point at which a cat breed is officially accepted under a cat fancy organization's rules. Registered

Cat - A cat registered through a recognized feline association that has documentation of its ancestry.

Registered Name - The official name used by a registered cat, which is typically long and reflective of its ancestry.

Registration - The record of the particulars of a cat's birth and ancestry filed with an official organization.

Scratching Post - A tower-like structure covered in carpet or rope that allows a cat to sharpen and clean its claws inside the house without being destructive to furniture.

Secondary Coat - In a cat, the fine hairs of the undercoat.

Semi-Longhair - Long-haired cats with a medium-length coat.

Shelter - Any local organization that exists for the purpose of rescuing and caring for homeless and stray animals. Also works to find permanent homes for these animals.

Show - An organized exhibition in which judges evaluate cats according to accepted standard for each breed and make awards accordingly.

Show Cat - Cats that participate in shows. Show Quality - Cats that meet the standards for their breed at a sufficient level to compete in organized cat shows.

Show Standard - A description of the ideal qualities of a breed of cats used as the basis for which the cats are judged in competition. Also known as standard of point.

Sire - The male member of a parenting set of cats.

Spay - The surgery to remove a female cat's ovaries.

Spray - A territorial behavior typically seen in male cats whereby the animal emits a stream of urine as a marker.

Stud - An intact male cat that has not been altered and is used as part of a breeding program.

Subcutaneous - Placed just below the skin, as in an injection.

Tapetum Lucidum - The interior portion of a cat's eye that aids in night vision and is highly reflective.

Undercoat - The layer of a cat's coat that is composed of down hairs.

Undercolor - The color of the hair lying closest to a cat's skin.

Vaccine - A weakened or dead preparation of a bacterium, virus, or other pathogen used to stimulate the production of antibodies for the purpose of creating immunity against the disease when injected.

Wean - The point at which a kitten begins to eat solid food and is taken off its mother's milk as the primary source of nutrition.

Whisker Break - Refers to an indentation of the upper jaw on a cat.

Whisker Pad - The thickened or fatty pads on either side of a cat's face holding rows of sensory whiskers.

Whole - A cat of either gender that is intact, and has not been neutered or spayed.

Glossary of Cat Terms

Index

Index

D

E

Index

Index

Index

Index

Index

Index

Photo Credits

Page 2, KrissiLundgren via Canva.com (Canva Pro License)

https://www.canva.com/photos/MAC8b5E0lVc-birman-cat/

Page 6, Sylvia_Adams via Canva.com (Canva Pro License)

https://www.canva.com/photos/MADAVS_HDD4-birman-cat/

Page 16, Lolostock via Canva.com (Canva Pro License)

https://www.canva.com/photos/MABV7N9yDC8-man-holding-his-birman-cat/

Page 27, v777999 via Canva.com (Canva Pro License)

https://www.canva.com/photos/MAED56gvvwE-cat-eating/

Page 43, Oleg Baliuk via Canva.com (Canva Pro License)

https://www.canva.com/photos/MAEX6U4O_SA-cat-having-groomed-inside-veterinary-clinic/

Page 48, Moncherie via Canva.com (Canva Pro License)

References

AZ Animals Staff 2022, accessed 7 March 2022, https://a-z-animals.com/animals/birman/#

Basepaws 2019, accessed 10 March 2022, https://basepaws.com/blogs/news/birman-cat-breed

Bioguard Corporation n.d, accessed 5 March 2022, https://www.bioguardlabs.com/breed-related-disease-birman-cat/

Bow Wow Meow Pet Insurance n.d, accessed 15 March 2022, https://bowwowinsurance.com.au/cats/cat-breeds/birman/

Catbreedslist.com n.d, accessed 10 March 2022, https://www.catbreedslist.com/all-cat-breeds/birman.html

Cattime n.d, accessed 24 March 2022, https://cattime.com/cat-breeds/birman-cats#/slide/1

Doug Jimerson and Claudia Guthrie 2021, Daily Paws, accessed 22 March 2022, https://www.dailypaws.com/cats-kittens/cat-breeds/birman

Emily Parker n.d, Catological, accessed 15 March 2022, https://www.catological.com/birman-facts/

Emily W. n.d, ASPCA Pet Health Insurance, accessed 8 March 2022, https://www.aspcapetinsurance.com/resources/birman/

Franny Syufy 2022, The Spruce Pets, accessed 22 March 2022, https://www.thesprucepets.com/cat-mating-and-reproduction-555437

References

Guild Group Holdings Limited n.d, accessed 5 March 2022,
https://vetschoice.guildinsurance.com.au/cats/cat-breeds/birman

Hillspet.com n.d, accessed 24 March 2022, https://www.hillspet.com/cat-care/cat-breeds/birman

Kayla Fratt 2019, The Spruce Pets, accessed 18 March 2022,
https://www.thesprucepets.com/birman-cat-full-profile-history-and-care-4693763

Kim Campbell Thornton 2019, Catster.com, accessed 5 March 2022,
https://www.catster.com/cats-101/all-about-the-birman-cat-breed

Lifetime Pet Cover Limited n.d, accessed 5 March 2022,
https://www.lifetimepetcover.co.uk/pet-advice/cat-breeds/birman/

Marye Audet n.d, LoveToKnow Media, accessed 26 March 2022,
https://cats.lovetoknow.com/Birman_Cats

Mentor Animal Hospital n.d, accessed 22 March 2022,
https://mentoranimalhospital.com/breeding-your-cat.pml#appointment-type

Nicole Cosgrove 2022, Pet Keen, accessed 18 March 2022,
https://petkeen.com/birman-cat/

Pet Culture Group 2021, accessed 10 March 2022,
https://www.petculture.com.au/breeds/birman-cat

Petbarn 2018, accessed 7 March 2022,
https://www.petbarn.com.au/petspot/cat/cat-breeds/birman-cat/

References

Petfinder n.d, accessed 5 March 2022, https://www.petfinder.com/cat-breeds/birman/

PetMD n.d, accessed 5 March 2022, https://www.petmd.com/cat/breeds/c_ct_birman

Petplan n.d, accessed 18 March 2022, https://www.petplan.co.uk/pet-information/cat/breed/birman/

Prestige Animal Hospital n.d, accessed 26 March 2022, https://www.prestigeanimalhospital.com/services/cats/breeds/birman

Purina n.d, accessed 25 March 2022, https://www.purina.co.uk/find-a-pet/cat-breeds/birman

Ryan Llera, BSc, DVM; Ernest Ward, DVM n.d, accessed 7 March 2022, https://vcahospitals.com/know-your-pet/breeding-and-queening-cats#:~:text=Pregnancy%20or%20gestation%20ranges%20from,will%20usually%20confirm%20her%20pregnancy.

Sainsbury's Bank n.d, accessed 10 March 2022, https://www.sainsburysbank.co.uk/pet-insurance/cat-breed/birman

Scrumbles n.d, accessed 5 March 2022, https://www.scrumbles.co.uk/birman-cat/

The Cat Fanciers' Association, Inc. n.d, accessed 18 March 2022, https://cfa.org/birman/

The Great Cat n.d, accessed 5 March 2022, https://www.thegreatcat.org/cat-breeds-and-species/birman-cat/

References

Tori Houle 2014, Pet Health Network, accessed 5 March 2022,
https://www.pethealthnetwork.com/cat-health/cat-breeds/fluffy-birman

VCA Animal Hospitals n.d, accessed 11 March 2022,
https://vcahospitals.com/know-your-pet/cat-breeds/birman

Vetsreet n.d, accessed 10 March 2022,
http://www.vetstreet.com/cats/birman#1_8jk7ll4g